NEW SERIES • VOLUME XXVI

COSTERUS

Rodopi

AMSTERDAM 1980

FROM COOPER TO PHILIP ROTH

Essays on American Literature

Presented to J.G. Riewald
on the occasion of
his seventieth birthday

Edited by J. Bakker and D.R.M. Wilkinson
with a foreword by J. Gerritsen

Printed in the Netherlands
ISBN: 90–6203–851–4

CONTENTS

FOREWORD

This volume brings together eight studies contributed by those of Jaap Riewald's colleagues who share with him an enthusiasm and — to varying degrees — a responsibility for the field which he has made first and foremost his own.

What it has thus lost in potential size (as a perusal of the *Tabula Gratulatorum* will quickly show) it has gained in appropriateness as a tribute to the doyen of American Literary studies in Holland at what must of necessity be a leave-taking, but is happily not to be a farewell.

A lifelong interest in education, married to a passion for careful and meticulous research are perhaps his most characteristic professional qualities. In adding that they make themselves equally felt in the composition of his wine cellar we touch on a side of his personality that is perhaps less fittingly honoured in a *Festschrift*, but to which a tribute should surely be paid.

While saying thank you in these pages, we hope we may long stay in his debt.

Johan Gerritsen

A PREFACE TO COOPER'S *THE LAST OF THE MOHICANS*

Though an international best-seller in his lifetime,[1] Cooper has been for long neglected by academic literary critics. A man who stood up unequivocally for the rights of landlords, who was proud to think of himself as an aristocrat, who dared to question the democratic value of one-man-one-vote, and who relentlessly attacked the standards of journalistic criticism - such a man is unlikely to attract the sympathies of the conventionally progressive American critical establishment. In the last two decades or so, Cooper has certainly attracted some attention, chiefly, one imagines, because there is a limit to what can be written about Hawthorne's melancholy or James's moral consciousness. But the general attitude to Cooper is usually patronizing, if not hostile. L. A. Fiedler's comments are representative: Cooper's "talent for invective and his moral intelligence were greater than his psychological insight or poetic skill ... he had all the qualifications for a great American writer except the simple ability to write." Fieldler's Tacitean epigram is followed by a contemptuous dismissal of *The Last of the Mohicans:*

> Were one of the actors to sweat or belch or retire to the bushes to relieve himself, the spell would be broken; we would know that all of them were flesh. But nothing gives the game away. The Indians talk like mythic Celts out of *Ossian,* the gentry like Fenimore Cooper remembering the genteel British novel, Hawkeye himself like an improbable blend of stage provincial, backwoods preacher, and instinctive sage. The novel is so all of a piece that reality does not intrude.[2]

The assumptions are clear. Cooper is not to be taken seriously as a novelist. If he is to be discussed at all, it is as a text for commentaries on the themes of sex, race, politics, environmental protection, the position of women, the role of the gentleman, myth-making, and so forth. G.Dekker, for instance, reduces *The Last of the Mohicans* to "issues:"

> Two things are at issue,then: whether miscegenation is a crime against nature, and, crime or no crime, whether a multiracial society in North America is possible.[3]

The very terminology, "miscegenation" and "multiracial society," is that of the modern *bien pensant;* it is certainly not Cooper's.

The two most valuable and sympathetic studies of Cooper, by Yvor Winters[4] and Marius Bewley,[5] who both stood well outside the

American critical establishment, do not pay much attention to *The Last of the Mohicans*. This is unfortunate, for it is, after all, upon *The Last of the Mohicans* that Cooper's conventional status as a popular classic depends. And if we are to come to a balanced judgement of that book, it is at least worth looking at "the words on the page," before abandoning it to the Freudians[6] and the Marxists.[7] Let us consider the novel in an old-fashioned way: what is the structure, the Aristotelian "arrangement of the incidents"?; what is the character development?; what is the quality of the prose? That such a simple task has not been undertaken before is in itself an indication of the state of Cooper criticism.

The title of *The Last of the Mohicans* has become part of the language and the novel itself has a special place in Cooper's voluminous *oeuvre*. The writing of the book was, as everybody knows, occasioned by an excursion that Cooper undertook with a party of young English aristocrats to the site of Glen's Falls in upstate New York. Cooper referred to the work as his most "intense" novel, and there is plenty of external evidence to indicate that he wrote it under considerable emotional pressure.[8] By 1825 the family estate had been irrevocably swallowed up in debt; his fine house at Fenimore, on the shores of Lake Otsego, had been destroyed by fire; and he had lost his only son. Novel-writing, which had hitherto been for him more or less a lucky sideline, seemed now to be forced on him as a permanent and unwelcome profession - all hopes of succeeding his father in the vocation of a gentleman farmer had gone. *The Last of the Mohicans* was written with the intensity of quiet desperation. If it failed, there was little future prospect of ever ridding himself of the constant crippling burden of debt. If it succeeded, he would be committed for life to a hazardous profession which in many ways was antipathetical to his deepest longings for a settled life in the country. *The Last of the Mohicans* was to be all or nothing; if it did not succeed, it was to be his last novel.[9]

The immediate inspiration, then, behind *The Last of the Mohicans,* was to show the young English aristocrats that America too has an ancestral history: a history of violence and slaughter and of human cross-purposes; a history of a precarious civilization built on the ruins of a shattered idyll of the primitive. Cooper's powerful evocation of the pathos of history is created out of virtually nothing: a few bare historical facts, some unreliable missionary narratives, and the vaguest of legends. Whereas Scott, at his best, breathed imaginative life into a mass of historical evidence, much of which he had himself collected and edited,[10] Cooper, as it were, had to create his own evidence; every detail depended on his own imaginative powers.

The story of *The Last of the Mohicans* is concerned with an episode in the "Old French War." In 1757 a party sets out from Fort Edward to reach Fort William Henry, which is besieged by the French under Montcalm. The party consists of two half-sisters, Alice and Cora Munro, daughters of the commander of Fort William Henry, who are escorted by Major Duncan Heyward, who is in love with Alice. They are accompanied by Magua, an Indian Huron guide, whose treachery soon becomes obvious, and by David Gamut, a psalm-singing Yankee music teacher. They meet

Hawkeye, the white hunter, and his two Indian friends, Chingachgook and his son Uncas, the last of the Mohicans. After various attacks from hostile Indians, they reach Fort William Henry only to find that Colonel Munro has been ordered to surrender to the French. After the surrender, the hostile Hurons massacre the defenceless occupants of the fort while Montcalm's troops stand powerlessly by: Alice and Cora are captured by Magua. Heyward, Munro, Hawkeye and his two Indian friends go in search of the girls; after many adventures, Alice is eventually rescued, but Cora and Uncas are killed. Such is the barest outline of the story.

The structure of the book fits perfectly into the exigencies of publication in double volume form. Volume I is concerned with the adventures *en route* between the two forts and culminates in the surrender of Fort William Henry, the ensuing massacre, and the capture by Magua of the two girls. Volume II is concerned with the search for the girls, and centres chiefly on adventures in the hostile Huron camp where Alice has been taken, and in the neutral Delaware camp where Cora has been left in safe custody by Magua. After the last chase and battle, Volume II closes with the elaborate ceremonial funeral of Cora and Uncas, which forms an almost operatic grand finale.[11]

All the hard facts, such as they are, are established in Volume I: the geographical background, the forests, rivers and lakes; the historical situation, relating to the war between the whites; and the ethnological characteristics of the Indian tribes. In Volume I the characters have to learn to operate within the constraints of that framework, and the experience is painful. Heywood, Gamut, Alice and Cora do not know how to cope with the forest; Hawkeye, Chingachgook and Uncas do not know how to cope with Heywood, Gamut, Alice and Cora; Montcalm does not know how to cope with Magua and his Indian allies. In Volume II a second cycle of events begins, in which the characters operate freely: they are "free" precisely because they have already been conditioned and educated to the exigencies of the historical environment. Cooper's use of such a structural technique is quite deliberate and most remarkable, if not unique.[12] For it is not only the characters who are conditioned and educated to the historical moment of the American frontier in 1757. We the readers, as we follow the characters in Volume I, are being conditioned and educated as well. When we come to the events of Volume II we accept, or we are meant to accept, the reality of Cooper's very special imaginative world. A dramatist needs an opening scene, or at most a first act, to establish the terms on which his play is to be understood. Most novelists need two or three opening chapters to mark out their selection from a recognizably familiar reality. Cooper realized that for his own very difficult artistic problem he needed half a book. Great art creates the terms by which it is understood.[13] The phenomenal success of *The Last of the Mohicans,* in both America and Europe, was a conclusive validation of Cooper's unusual procedure, so that when, fifteen years later, he came to write the final novels in the Leatherstocking series *The Pathfinder* (1840) and *The Deerslayer* (1841), he could assume a conditioned audience, and adopt a unitary structure which enabled him to write with a completely free imaginative flow. He could by then be confident that he had established an acceptable and "real" world.

In *The Last of the Mohicans,* a striking example of the historical education of the reader is in Chapters XII and XIII. After a bloody engagement with the Hurons, Hawkeye and his party refresh themselves at a mineral spring which was, by 1826, to become the site of a famous spa, Ballston Springs:

> each of the foresters stooped and took a parting draught at that solitary and silent spring, around which within fifteen years the wealth, beauty and talents of a hemisphere were to assemble in throngs, in pursuit of health and pleasure ... The whole party moved swiftly through the narrow path, towards the north, leaving the healing waters to mingle unheeded with the adjacent brook, and the bodies of the dead to fester on the neighboring mount, without the rites of sepulture (XII, 141).[14]

But the history of the forest not only looks forward from 1757, it also looks back. Half a day's journey onward from the spring, the travellers settle for the night at a deserted blockhouse where Hawkeye in his youth had fought with the Mohicans against the Delawares. Hawkeye tells the story to Heyward, Alice and Cora:

> 'I was then young, and new to the sight of blood; and not relishing the thought that creatures who had spirits like myself should lay on the naked ground, to be torn asunder by beasts, or to bleach in the rain, I buried the dead with my own hands, under that very hillock where you have placed yourselves; and no bad seat does it make either, though it be raised by the bones of mortal men.'
>
> Heyward and the sisters arose, on the instant, from the grassy sepulchre; nor could the two latter, notwithstanding the terrific scenes they had so recently passed through, entirely suppress an emotion of natural horror, when they found themselves in such familiar contact with the grave of the dead Mohawks. The gray light, the gloomy little area of dark grass, surrounded by its border of brush, beyond which the pines rose, in breathing silence apparently into the very clouds, and the deathlike stillness of the vast forest, were all in unison to deepen such a sensation.
>
> 'They are gone, and they are harmless,' continued Hawkeye, waving his hand, with a melancholy smile, at their manifest alarm ... 'And of all those who aided in placing them where they lie, Chingachgook and I only are living! The brothers and family of the Mohican formed our war party; and you see before you all that are now left of his race' (XIII, 145).

The reaction of Heyward and the girls, in jumping up when they find that they are sitting on a pile of dead Indians, is of course faintly grotesque; but so too, by implication, are the civilized airs and graces of the visitors to Ballston Spa in 1826. Furthermore, the incident has its ironies within the story itself. The young and innocent Hawkeye used to provide dead Indians with a decent burial; but now, in 1757, he leaves them to rot and fester.

By the end of Volume I the fictional characters are caught up in the historical reality, Montcalm's siege of Fort William Henry. Montcalm is affable, courteous, and combines "a frank and easy air" with "a little hauteur" (XV, 179); in arranging terms for the surrender of the fort, he is "a liberal enemy" (XVI 193). Munro only surrenders when he has been ordered to do so by his superior commander, General Webb, and Montcalm allows honorable terms. After signing the articles of surrender, Montcalm has a secret meeting with his Huron ally, the treacherous Magua, and tries to persuade him to restrain the Hurons from any violence towards the defenceless occupants of the fort. Magua promises reluctantly, but Montcalm has his doubts:

> Montcalm lingered long and melancholy ... brooding deeply on the temper which his ungovernable ally had just discovered ... As he mused he became keenly sensible of the deep responsibility they assume, who disregard the means to attain their end, and of all the danger of setting in motion an engine which it exceeds human power to control (XVII, 199-220).

In the ensuing massacre after the surrender, the French troops stand idly by. There was an historical fact, and Cooper lays the blame fairly and squarely on Montcalm. But Cooper the novelist has prepared us for the historical fact by a fictional incident which engages our emotional sympathies in a contrary direction. In Chapter XIV, Heyward and his party have to pass through the French lines. They suddenly encounter a young French sentry. Heyward, accompanied by Alice and Cora boldly approaches him; Heyward poses as a French officer who has captured the two girls.[15] Civilities and courtesies are exchanged. The young Frenchman commiserates with the girls and assures them that they will be well treated by Montcalm. Cora wishes the young soldier well; the Frenchman gallantly acknowledges her kind remarks; Heyward wishes him "Bonne nuit, mon camerade;" and as they pass on they hear him singing a romantic song, "recalled to his mind by the sight of women and perhaps by recollections of his own distant and beautiful France." A few moments later a groan and a splash are heard. Chingachgook, the Mohican chief, rejoins the party:

> With one hand he attached the reeking scalp of the unfortunate young Frenchman to his girdle, and with the other he replaced the knife and tomahawk that had drunk his blood. He then took his wonted station, with the air of a man who believed he had done a deed of merit.
>
> Hawkeye ... stood musing in profound silence. Then shaking his head in a mournful manner, he muttered,
>
> ''Twould have been a cruel and inhuman act for a white-skin; but 'tis the gift and natur' of an Indian, and I suppose it should not be denied. I could wish, though, it had befallen an accursed Mingo, rather than that gay young boy from the old countries.'
>
> 'Enough!' said Heyward ... ''tis done; and though better it were left undone, cannot be amended' (XIV, 159).

It is significant that it is Hawkeye, the friend of Chingachgook and a man of the woods who is inured to such things, who expressly laments the deed, and it is Heyward, the officer, who is eager to pass it over.[16]

The relationship between Volume I and Volume II comes out most strikingly if we consider the development and change in the characters: there is development in the sense that a character extends its potentialities within the limitations of the original data; and there is change in the sense that a character comes to be regarded quite differently by the other characters and by the reader.

The most striking instance of character change is David Gamut. He is the first character to be described in detail (indeed his physical description is the most elaborate of all the characters), and the reader might be forgiven for assuming, at the outset, that the major theme of the novel was to be the adventures in the forest of the music teacher, with his twenty-sixth edition of the Bay Psalm Book and his pitch-pipe:

> His head was large; his shoulders narrow; his arms long and dangling; while his hands were small, if not delicate. His legs and thighs were thin, nearly to emaciation, but of extraordinary length ... A sky-blue coat, with short and broad skirts, and low cape, exposed a long thin neck ... A large, civil cocked hat, like those worn by clergymen within the last thirty years, surmounted the whole, furnishing dignity to a good-natured and somewhat vacant countenance, that apparently needed such artificial aid, to support the gravity of some high and extraordinary trust (I, 8).

Once in the forest, however, this portentous figure is reduced to a comic butt. Gamut is at first regarded by Heyward and Hawkeye with scarcely disguised contempt. But Hawkeye's attitude to Gamut is already ambivalent. Though he makes fun of the awkward Yankee's helplessness, he commiserates with him on the necessary slaughter of his horse; and when the party are besieged in the cavern at Glen's Falls, it is only Hawkeye who is affected by Gamut's psalmsinging:

> The Indians riveted their eyes to the rocks, and listened with an attention that seemed to turn them to stone. But Hawkeye, who had placed his chin in his hand, with an expression of cold indifference, gradually suffered his rigid features to relax, until, as verse succeeded verse, he felt his iron nature subdued, while his recollection was carried back to boyhood, when his ears had been accustomed to listen to similar sounds of praise, in the settlements of the colony. His roving eyes began to moisten, and before the hymn was ended, scalding tears rolled out of fountains that had long seemed dry (VI, 60).

But the emotion lasts only a moment, and the hymn is abruptly terminated by the horrific war-cry of the Hurons outside, which is a preliminary to the ensuing violent action.

In Chapter XII, after the Hurons have been temporarily repulsed,

Gamut and Hawkeye enter into a fierce dispute on the subject of predestination, and Hawkeye counters Gamut's appeal to the Bible "with singular and ill-concealed disdain;" Hawkeye's only Book is the Book of Nature. When David Gamut begins a hymn of thanksgiving for safe deliverance, he now gets no emotional response whatsoever:

> Hawkeye listened, while he coolly adjusted his flint and reloaded his rifle; but the sounds ... failed to awaken his slumbering emotions. Never minstrel, or by whatever more suitable name David should be known, drew upon his talents in the presence of more insensible auditors; though considering the singleness and sincerity of his motive, it is probable that no bard of profane song ever uttered notes that ascended so near to the throne where all homage and praise is due (XII, 135).

In the absence of response from Hawkeye, Cooper has redressed the balance by a brief and pious authorial intrusion; Hawkeye's natural religion is firmly "placed," and it is clear that neither Hawkeye nor Gamut are the mouthpieces of the novelist.

At the end of Volume I, in the confusion of the massacre at the fort, the figure of Gamut, though "helpless and useless," predominates. He refuses to desert the two sisters, and stands over them unmoved, singing psalms at the top of his voice. This certainly saves the two girls from death, for the bloodthirsty Hurons are arrested by the sight:

> More than one savage rushed towards them, thinking to rifle the unprotected sisters of their attire, and bear away their scalps; but when they found this strange and unmoved figure riveted to his post, they paused to listen. Astonishment soon changed to admiration, and they passed on to other, and less courageous victims, openly expressing their satisfaction at the firmness with which the white warrior sang his death song. Encouraged and deluded by his success, Gamut exerted all his powers to extend what he believed so holy an influence (XVII, 208).

The reader is not allowed, for more than a moment, to be deluded into believing in the miraculous powers of the Bay Psalm Book. The strange sound of Gamut's singing has the unfortunate effect of drawing the attention of the evil Magua to the two girls, whom he had been searching for in the general *mêlée*. Magua carries off Alice and Cora; and Gamut, "perceiving that he was left alone, utterly disregarded as a subject too worthless even to destroy," voluntarily follows the two sisters into captivity.

Volume II opens with Heyward, Munro, Hawkeye and two Mohicans, trying to find the tracks of Magua and his prisoners. It is Gamut's pitch-pipe, dangling from a thorn bush, that puts them on the trail. Hawkeye does not conceal his patronizing scorn for Gamut:

> ''Tis the tooting we'pon of the singer! now we shall have a trail a priest might travel,' Hawkeye said ... 'I begin to have some hopes of the fellow, since he has given up squalling to follow some better trade.'

> 'At least he has been faithful to his trust,' said Heyward, 'and Cora and Alice are not without a friend.'
> 'Yes,' said Hawkeye, dropping his rifle and leaning on it with an air of visible contempt, 'he will do their singing! Can he slay a buck for their dinner, journey by the moss on the beeches, or cut the throat of a Huron?' (XVIII, 220).

Then, when the rescue party approach the Huron camp, the first person they encounter is a fantastic Indian figure:

> It was impossible to discover the expression of his features, through the grotesque mask of paint under which they were concealed ... His head was shaved, as usual, with the exception of the crown, from whose tuft three or four faded feathers from a hawk's wing were loosely dangling ... His legs were bare, and sadly cut and torn by briers. The feet were, however, covered with a pair of good deer-skin moccasins. Altogether, the appearance of the individual was forlorn and miserable (XXI, 260).

The figure turns out to be Gamut who is considered by the Hurons to be mad because of his psalm singing; they have dressed him accordingly as a fool and allowed him to wander at will through the camp and the forest, for the Indians (like the Russians) have a great respect for holy fools. Hawkeye treats the discovery of Gamut as a huge joke, "the Indians never harm a non-composser" (XXII, 265), but when Hawkeye asks why Gamut did not try to make his way back from Fort William Henry to the safety of Fort Edward, Gamut explains, in his own quaint vocabulary, that he has determined not to lose contact with Alice and Cora:

> 'Though my soul would rejoice to visit the habitations of Christendom once more, my feet would rather follow the tender spirits intrusted to my keeping ... than take one step backward, while they pined in captivity and sorrow' (XXII, 265).

The admiration for Gamut of the two Mohicans, Uncas and Chingachgook, is direct, unqualified and generous. Hawkeye's response, by contrast, seems mean and tiresome. He restores to Gamut the pitch-pipe, but not without some variations on his constant "he-man-in-the-great-outdoors" theme which, in this particular context, sounds peculiarly hollow and distasteful:

> Though the figurative language of Gamut was not very intelligible, the sincere and steady expression of his eye, and the glow on his honest countenance, were not easily mistaken. Uncas pressed closer to his side, and regarded the speaker with a look of commendation, while his father expressed his satisfaction by the ordinary pithy exclamation of approbation. Hawkeye shook his head as he rejoined.
> 'The Lord never intended that the man should place all his endeavours in his throat, to the neglect of other and better gifts! But he has fallen into the hands of some silly woman, when he should have been gathering his education under a blue sky, among the beauties of the forest' (XXII, 266).

The Gamut-Hawkeye relationship undergoes further developments. In Chapter XXVI, when Alice is being rescued from the Huron camp, Hawkeye's only chance of escape is to borrow Gamut's madman's clothing and to ask Gamut to remain behind in the hope that, as a "non-composser," the Hurons will refrain from killing him. Gamut consents to the proposal. Hawkeye thinks to console him by guaranteeing that, if Gamut is scalped, he will be revenged. Against this suggestion, Gamut most vigorously protests:

> 'Hold!' said Gamut ... 'I am an unworthy and humble follower of One who taught not the damnable principle of revenge. Should I fall, therefore, seek no victims to my manes, but rather forgive my destroyers; and if you remember them at all, let it be in prayers for the enlightenment of their minds, and for their external welfare.'
>
> Hawkeye hesitated, and appeared to muse.
>
> 'There is a principle in that,' he said, 'different from the law of the woods; and yet it is fair and noble to reflect upon.' Then, heaving a heavy sigh, probably among the last he ever drew in pining for a condition he had so long abandoned, he added, 'It is what I would wish to practice myself, as one without a cross of blood, though it is not always easy to deal with an Indian as you would with a fellow Christian. God bless you, friend; I do believe your scent is not greatly wrong, when the matter is duly considered, and keeping eternity before the eyes, though much depends on the natural gifts, and the force of temptation'.
>
> So saying, Hawkeye returned and shook Gamut cordially by the hand (XXVI, 327).

Gamut's protest here brings out a new dimension in Hawkeye, even if it is somewhat hedged around with situational ethics.

But by the time of the last battle, the final assault against the Hurons to rescue Cora, David Gamut (now referred to by Hawkeye as "the honest fellow") has himself undergone a character development. Hawkeye tells Gamut that he may wait behind for five minutes and all will be over in the final charge. But Gamut determines to join the fight and, though he cannot handle a rifle, he has armed himself, like his namesake David, with a sling. Hawkeye looks upon the sling "with a cold and discouraging eye," but consents to allow Gamut to participate in the final charge:

> 'it seems to be your gift to go unharmed amid fire; and as you have hitherto been favoured - singer, you can follow; we may find use for you in the shoutings!
>
> 'I thank you friend,' returned David, supplying himself, like his royal namesake, from among the pebbles of the brook; 'though not given to the desire to kill, had you sent me away, my spirit would have been troubled' (XXXII, 391).

But it is in the concluding funeral scene that Gamut comes into his own. It is only he, and not Heyward or Hawkeye, who can offer any consolation to Munro, the bereaved father. And after the Deleware maidens have sung their death chants for Uncas and Cora, it is

Hawkeye who calls upon them to listen to David Gamut as "one who better knows the Christian fashions:"

> The females stood modestly aside, and, from having been the principal actors in the scene, they now became the meek and attentive observers of that which followed. During the time David was occupied in pouring out the pious feelings of his spirit in this manner, not a sign of surprise, nor a look of impatience, escaped them. They listened like those who knew the meaning of the strange words, and appeared as if they felt the mingled emotions of sorrow, hope, and resignation, they were intended to convey.
>
> Excited by the scene he had just witnessed, and perhaps influenced by his own secret emotions, the master of song exceeded his usual efforts. His full, rich voice was not found to suffer by a comparison with the soft tones of the girls; and his more modulated strains possessed, at least for the ears of those to whom they were peculiarly addressed, the additional power of intelligence. He ended the anthem, as he had commended it, in the midst of a grave and solemn stillness (XXXIII, 415).

Another character who undergoes radical change is Major Duncan Heyward. In Volume I he is the gallant but rather stiff and conventional soldier, dutifully attentive to Alice and Cora, but utterly unaccustomed to the business of skirmishing with Indians in the forest. His sentimentalizings over the beauties of the scenery are rudely cut short by the girls themselves:

> 'Here is nothing to be seen but the gloom and quiet of a lovely evening', whispered Duncan, 'how much should we prize such a scene, and all this breathing solitude, at any other moment, Cora! Fancy yourselves in security and what now, perhaps, increases your terror, may be made conducive to enjoyment'-
>
> 'Listen!' interrupted Alice (VII, 67).

At the first onset of the Hurons at Glen's Falls, Heyward attempts to rescue a drowning Indian, but is firmly held back by Hawkeye:

> The first generous impulse of Heyward was to rush to the rescue of the hapless wretch; but he felt himself bound to the spot by the iron grasp of the immovable scout (VII, 74).

But when the Hurons make their first attack, physical restraint is no longer necessary:

> Heyward felt a burning desire to rush forward to meet them, so intense was the delirious anxiety of the moment; but he was restrained by the deliberate examples of Hawkeye and Uncas (VII, 75).

Heyward remains what he is, even at the opening of Volume II. As the party searching for Alice and Cora are escaping down the river in a canoe paddled by Uncas and Chingachgook, Hawkeye orders Heyward and Munro to lie down to escape the Hurons' bullets, but Heyward refuses:

> 'It would be an ill example for the highest in rank to dodge, while the warriors were under fire!'
> 'Lord! Lord! That is now a white man's courage!' exclaimed the scout; 'and like too many of his notions, not to be maintained by reason. Do you think Chingachgook, or Uncas, or even I, who am a man without a cross, would deliberate about finding cover in the skrimmage, when an open body would do no good?'
> ...
> 'All that you say is very true, my friend, 'replied Heyward, 'still, our customs must prevent us from doing as you wish!'

The argument is interrupted by a volley of rifle-fire from the bank, and Uncas turns round to look at Heyward sitting upright in the canoe:

> The countenance of Uncas expressed no other emotion, as Heyward was compelled to think, than amazement at finding men willing to encounter so useless an exposure. Chingachgook was probably better acquainted with the notions of white men, for he did not even cast a glance aside from the riveted look his eye maintained on the object by which he governed their course (XX, 246).

So much for Major Heyward as Beau Geste.

But it is when Alice is eventually located in the Huron camp that Heyward undergoes a change that is both real and symbolic. Having discovered that Gamut passes unscathed among the Hurons because he is considered to be mad, Heyward demands to be allowed to penetrate the Huron camp in disguise:

> 'I too can play the madman, the fool, the hero: in short, any or everything to rescue her I love. Name your objections no longer; I am resolved ... You have the means of disguise; change me; paint me too, if you will; in short, alter me to anything - a fool' (XXII, 270).

At first Hawkeye objects to the plan, but eventually, "with a good humored smile," allows Chingachgook to transform the military-looking appearance of Heyward into "a natural fool and a buffoon." When Heyward has been painted and disguised, Hawkeye gazes at him "in open admiration," wishes him well in his adventure into the enemy camp, and promises to revenge him if he fails and is scalped:

> 'I say, young gentleman, may Providence bless your undertaking ... and remember that to outwit the knaves it is lawful to practise things that may not be naturally the gift of a white man' (XXII, 272).

And so, led by Gamut the natural fool, Heyward sets off on his dangerous mission. The echoes of *King Lear,* with Edgar as Poor Tom accompanying the Fool, are surely obvious. But even without that background resonance, the episode shows Cooper using 'poetic' devices in a way that is entirely new in the history of the American or the English novel. Cooper may be unable to achieve any complexity in the inward development of his characters, and Heyward is a 'stock' character if ever there was one, but we must not deny Cooper's efforts to achieve complexity by outward means. Heyward, demanding to be made to look like a fool, and submitting to having his face painted by Chingachgook, presents us, in all the economy of art, with the confusing ironies of class, profession and race.

As for the Indian characters, the two Mohicans, Chingachgook and Uncas, undergo little change or development; even Uncas's affection for Cora is virtually inarticulate. It is the character of Magua, the villainous Huron, that undergoes the most striking development. In Volume I he is the stage-villain. He is determined to revenge himself on Munro by making Cora his squaw, but all he does is to roll his eyes, gnash his teeth, and show "cunning," "disdain," and "cold malignancy." Apart from one rabble-rousing speech, he is as inarticulate as Uncas. But in Volume II he appears in a different dimension. After Alice has escaped from the Huron camp, Magua has to prevent the Hurons from attacking the Delaware camp, where Cora has been left for safe keeping, and he has to reassert his power as leader over his somewhat dejected supporters. His motives are entirely personal, and Cooper endows him with a kind of intelligence that is not given to Chingachgook or Uncas. It is the intelligence, in fact, of a certain species of white man; but just as we are about to say that this is a 'superior' intelligence Cooper makes it clear, with heavy authorial sarcasm, that it is the intelligence of a party political manager:

> He commenced by flattering the self-love of his auditors; a never-failing method of commanding attention ... Then he spoke of their necessities; of the gifts they had a right to expect for their past services; of their distance from their proper hunting-grounds and native villages; and of the necessity of consulting prudence more, and inclination less, in so critical circumstances. When he perceived that, while the old men applauded his moderation, many of the fiercest and most distinguished of the warriors listened to these politic plans with lowering looks, he cunningly led them back to the subject which they most loved. He spoke openly of the fruits of their wisdom, which he boldly pronounced would be a complete and final triumph over their enemies... In short, he so blended the warlike with the artful, the obvious with the obscure, as to flatter the propensities of both parties, and to leave to each a subject for hope, while neither could say it clearly comprehended his intentions.
>
> The orator, or the politician, who can produce such a state of things, is commonly popular with his contemporaries, however he may be treated by posterity. All perceived that more was meant than was uttered, and each one believed that the hidden meaning was precisely such as his own faculties enabled him to understand, or his own wishes led him to anticipate.
>
> In this happy state of things, it is not surprising that the management of Magua prevailed (XXVII, 337).

Having gained his purposes and regained his leadership of the tribe,

Magua retires to his tent to brood like a Miltonic Satan.

When Magua goes to the Delaware camp to argue for the surrender of Cora, his character obtains a further dimension. He convinces Tamenund, the Delaware sage, of his peaceful intentions, by a speech which invokes the primitive Indian tribal idyll, so dear to Tamenund's heart. Unlike Magua's previous speech to the Hurons, which was presented in *oratio obliqua* almost like a piece of parliamentary reporting by a hostile journalist, Magua's speech to the Delawares is rendered by Cooper in direct 'poetic' prose:

> 'Some the Great Spirit made with skins brighter and redder than yonder sun ... and these did He fashion to his own mind. He gave them this island as He had made it, covered with trees, and filled with game. The wind made their clearings; the sun and rains ripened their fruits; and the snows came to tell them to be thankful. What need had they of roads to journey by! They saw through the hills! When the beavers worked, they lay in the shade, and looked on. The winds cooled them in summer; in winter, skins kept them warm. If they fought among themselves, it was to prove that they were men. They were brave; they were just; they were happy' (XXIX, 360).

In this speech Cooper is deliberately trying to create an acceptable imaginative model of nostalgic Indian rhetoric by combining a vocabulary of elemental simplicity with a strong metrical structure. If one must talk of sources, then it may be said that Cooper combines Shakespearean blank verse ("What need had they of roads to journey by") with the pastoral atmosphere of Virgil's *Eclogues* (which Cooper knew by heart from his schooldays). What it most clearly does *not* derive from, *pace* L.A. Fielder, is *Ossian*.[17] Magua's speech on this occasion is quite different in style from Tamenund's answer to Cora, a few moments later:

> 'I know that the pale-faces are a proud and hungry race, I know that they claim not only to have the earth, but that the meanest of their color is better than the Sachems of the red-man. The dogs and crows of their tribes ... would bark and caw before they would take a woman to their wigwams whose blood was not of the color of snow. But let them not boast before the face of the Manitou too loud. They entered the land at the rising, and may yet go off at the setting sun. I have often seen the locusts strip the leaves from the trees, but the season of blossoms has always come again' (XXIX, 365).

Tamenund's speech is rational, not emotive, but is imaginatively acceptable as 'foreign' by being couched in the gnomic antithetical sententiousness of a recognizable 'folk' language. It is wholly unfair to the seriousness of Cooper's artistic endeavours to assume that his Indians speak all the same way. Such a criticism could be much more validly applied to Hemingway's Spaniards in *For Whom the Bell Tolls*.

The themes of sex and race in *The Last of the Mohicans* have occupied so much critical attention that a third, and equally important theme, eschatology, has been almost entirely neglected. Cooper quite simply believed that men's actions on earth were largely determined by their belief in what happened after death, and that was one reason why Indians behave differently from white men, and why Hawkeye behaves differently from Gamut. Perhaps the reason why contemporary critics have passed over this most obvious point in *The Last of the Mohicans* is because contemporary novels are, alas, concerned far more often with scatology than with eschatology.

In Volume I, Hawkeye's argument with Gamut on the subject of predestination, which has already been discussed in this essay, is the most important cause of Hawkeye's initial hostility to Gamut. Then, at the opening of Volume II, when Hawkeye and Major Heyward return at night to the ruins of Fort William Henry, Hawkeye holds forth on the subject of the after life, interrupted only by the strange noises of the forest:

> 'Speaking of spirits, Major, are you of opinion that the heaven of a red-skin and of us whites will be one and the same?'
>
> 'No doubt - no doubt.'
>
> 'For my own part,'continued Hawkeye, 'I believe that paradise is ordained for happiness; and that men will be indulged in it according to their dispositions and gifts. I therefore judge that a red-skin is not far from the truth when he believes he is to find them glorious hunting-grounds of which his traditions tell; nor, for that matter, do I think it would be any disparagement to a man without a cross to pass his time ... I have heard preachers say, in the settlements, that heaven was a place of rest. Now men's minds differ as to their ideas of enjoyment. For myself, and I say it with reverence to the ordering of Providence, it would be no great indulgence to be kept shut up in those mansions of which they preach, having a natural longing for motion and the chase.'
>
> 'It is difficult to account for the feelings that may attend the last great change,' said Heyward.
>
> 'It would be a change, indeed, for a man who has passed his days in the open air,' returned the single-minded scout; 'and who has so often broken his fast on the head waters of the Hudson, to sleep within sound of the roaring Mohawk. But it is a comfort to know we serve a merciful Master, though we do it each after his fashion, and with great tracts of wilderness atween us' (XIX, 226).

This episode is clearly a preparation for the final burial scene of Cora and Uncas. The funeral is obviously a 'set-piece,' and Cooper has arranged it with consciously formal artistry. Munro stands by the bier of Cora; Chingachgook stands by the bier of Uncas; Alice and Heyward stand together; Hawkeye stands alone; and to complete the pattern, an *aide-de-camp* of Montcalm appears in the background. As the sun goes down, Tamenund begins the funeral ceremonies, and his words are a cue for the chant by a choir of Delaware maidens. Contrary to what we might have expected, Cooper renders the song of the Delaware maidens in indirect speech. By this device the white mourners are excluded from the full significance of the

Indian rites - apart from Hawkeye, who understands the language; and we the readers have also a sense of sharing Hawkeye's secret knowledge:

> Others again, in due succession, spoke to Cora herself, in the low, soft language of tenderness and love. They exhorted her to be of cheerful mind, and to fear nothing for her future welfare. A hunter would be her companion, who knew how to provide for her smallest wants; and a warrior was at her side who was able to protect her against every danger. They promised that her path should be pleasant, and her burden light. They cautioned her against unavailing regrets for the friends of her youth, and the scenes where her fathers had dwelt; assuring her that the 'blessed hunting-grounds of Lenape' contained vales as pleasant, streams as pure, and flowers as sweet, as the 'heaven of the pale-faces' ... Then, in a wild burst of their chant, they sang with united voices the temper of the Mohican's mind. They pronounced him noble, manly, and generous; all that became a warrior, and all that a maid might love ... He was of a race that had once been lords on the shores of the salt lake, and his wishes had led him back to a people who dwelt about the graves of his fathers. Why should not such a predilection be encouraged! That she was of a blood purer and richer than the rest of her nation, any eye might have seen; that she was equal to the dangers and daring of a life in the woods, her conduct had proved; and now, they added, the 'wise one of the earth' had transplanted her to a place where she would find congenial spirits, and might be forever happy.
>
> Then, with another transition in voice and subject, allusions were made to Alice, the virgin who wept in the adjacent lodge. They compared her to flakes of snow; as pure, as white, as brilliant, and as liable to melt in the fierce heats of summer, or congeal in the frosts of winter. They doubted not that she was lovely in the eyes of the young chief, whose skin and whose sorrow seemed so like her own ... they denied her no meed her rare charms might properly claim. Her ringlets were compared to the exuberant tendrils of the vine, her eye to the blue vault of the heavens, and the most spotless cloud, with its glowing flush of the sun, was admitted to be less attractive than her bloom (XXXIII, 410).

This is immediately followed by David Gamut's performance of the Christian obsequies, which forms a striking contrast in artistic effect. Cooper gives Gamut no actual words at all, in direct or indirect speech, only a description of the musical quality of his song. By this device the Indians are able, as it were, to 'understand' him and to share his feelings.[18]

And then, when the illusion of sympathetic unity between Indians and whites is at its most profound, Cooper deliberately breaks the spell:

> Munro seemed sensible that the time was come for him to exert what is, perhaps, the greatest effort of which human nature is

> capable. He bared his gray locks, and looked around the timid and quiet throng by which he was encircled with a firm and collected countenance. Then motioning with his hand for the scout to listen, he said, -
>
> 'Say to these kind and gentle females, that a heartbroken and failing man returns them his thanks. Tell them, that the Being we all worship, under different names, will be mindful of their charity; and that the time shall not be distant when we may assemble around his throne without distinction of sex, or rank, or colour'...
>
> 'To tell them this,' said Hawkeye, 'would be to tell them that the snows come not in the winter, or that the sun shines fiercest when the trees are stripped of their leaves.'
>
> Then turning to the women, he made such a communication of the other's gratitude as he deemed most suited to the capacities of his listeners (XXXIII, 416).

Hawkeye's reply to Munro, in direct speech, is still poetic and *exaltê,* even though its content is negative:

> 'To tell them this would be to tell them that the snows come not in winter, or that the sun shines fiercest when the trees are stripped of their leaves.'

It is the subsequent abrupt resumption of the narrative, in polysyllabic prose of a Daniel Websterish orotundity, that brutally and irrevocably shatters the illusion and returns us to a Conradian world of human misunderstandings and cross-purposes:

> turning to the women, he made such a communication of the other's gratitude as he deemed most suited to the capacities of his listeners.

When the exigencies of the novel demand it, there is no doubt that Cooper is capable of using the arts of language for his creative purposes.

In the opening of *The Wing and Wing,* Cooper complains that European readers obtain their factual information "through works of *a light character, similar to this of our own.*"[19] Like Trollope, Cooper always publicly adopted an apologetic and deprecatory attitude towards the actual business of writing novels and, like Trollope, he has suffered in consequence from critics who have taken him at his word. But whether the act of writing was easy or difficult, carelessly or carefully done, is irrelevant to a critical consideration of the final product. Cooper may have thought that he was accepting light fiction, and the narrative of adventure as a substantive genre, and merely adding to it an instructive element; but in fact he transformed the genre. He was not a literary innocent by any means: he was steeped in Shakespearean drama and had a lively sense of Romantic poetry. His intensely independent intellectual powers, coupled with his profoundly serious and complex approach to life, had to create a new genre if they were to express themselves in fiction at all. *The Last of the Mohicans* is the first unqualified example in the

English language of "the novel as dramatic poem,"[20] If Cooper's novels deserve to be taken seriously, they deserve to be read as closely and as critically as we would read the novels of Hawthorne, James, or Conrad. Cooper's novels are not merely creations of myth, or expressions of unfashionable political and social ideas. If they have any value as literature they should be able to stand the traditional tests of imaginative art.

University of Nijmegen T.A. Birrell

NOTES

1 See J.G. Riewald, "The Translational Reception of American Literature in Europe 1800-1900: A Review of Research," *English Studies* 60 (1979), 565-9.
2 L.A. Fiedler, *Love and Death in the American Novel* (London, 1970; 1st. ed. New York, 1960), pp. 169, 179, 188.
3 G. Dekker, *James Fenimore Cooper the Novelist* (London, 1967), p. 71.
4 In *Maule's Curse* (1938).
5 In *The Eccentric Design* (1959), first published in part in *Scrutiny* (1952-3).
6 For a female Freudian, Hawkeye's rifle is "his one objective phallic emblem" - his subjective phallic emblems are left mercifully to the imagination (see Annette Kolodny, "Love and Sexuality in *The Pathfinder*," in Wayne Fields, ed., *James Fenimore Cooper: a Collection of Critical Essays*, Englewood Cliffs, 1979).
7 The approach to Cooper of the Hungarian Marxist Georg Lukács, originally published in Moscow in 1937 under Stalin's Terror, is predictable: the Leatherstocking tales describe the destruction of a primitive by a bourgeois society, and Leatherstocking himself is the man in the middle. (See G. Lukács, *The Historical Novel*, London, 1962).
8 J.F. Beard (ed.), *The Letters and Journals of James Fenimore Cooper* (Cambridge, Mass., 1960), vol. I, p. 131. Susan Cooper tells us that her father suffered from an attack of sunstroke while writing Chapter XII. To judge from Cooper's own description of his symptoms during later attacks of the same illness, it would seem that "sunstroke" was a nineteenth-century euphemism for acute diarrhoea. For a treatment of Cooper's novels as the basis for psycho-analytic biography, with reference to "psychic needs," "libidinal attachments," "libidinal desires," "a psychic axis," "a mild form of paranoia," *et hoc genus omne*, see S. Railton, *Fenimore Cooper: a Study of his Life and Imagination* (Princeton, 1978).
9 J.F. Beard, *op. cit.*, p. 120.
10 H.R. Trevor-Roper, *The Romantic Movement and the Study of History* (London, 1969), p. 7. The whole of this brilliant essay is full of insights for the literary critic.
11 H. Daniel Peck, *A World by Itself: the Pastoral Moment in Cooper's Fiction* (New Haven, 1977), Chapters 7 and 8, offers a very

elaborate and schematic comparison between Volumes I and II. William Charvat made the essential points about Cooper's two volume structure in his introduction to the Riverside Edition of *The Last of the Mohicans* (Boston, 1958), and in his essay "Cooper as Professional Author" in H.M. Jones (ed.), *James Fenimore Cooper: a Re-appraisal* (Cooperstown, 1954). In R.E. Spiller and Philip C. Blackburn, *A Descriptive Bibliography of the Writings of James Fenimore Cooper* (New York, 1934), no indication of the volume divisions is given.

12 Any comparable 50-50 division of a novel, in English or American literature, is unknown to me.

13 This seems to me a more valid observation than Eliot's "genuine poetry can communicate before it is understood." *Selected Essays* (London, 1934), p. 238.

14 All page references to Cooper's novels are to the "Leather-stocking" edition, published by Routledge, London, 1883-89.

15 In case the hypercritical reader may complain that such an incident is highly improbable, it may be worth pointing out that at the siege of Quebec, two years later, it was the French pronunciation of a Scottish officer which enabled General Wolfe to elude the French sentries and scale the Heights of Abraham. See F. Parkman, *Montcalm and Wolfe* (London, 1964), p. 550.

16 T. Martin, "From the Ruins of History: *The Last of the Mohicans*" (reprinted in Wayne Fields, ed., *James Fenimore Cooper: a Collection of Critical Essays,* Englewood Cliffs 1979, pp. 80-90), refers to this episode but draws different conclusions.

17 The following is a representative sample from Macpherson's *Ossian:*

> A light fell on the soul of the maid: it rose kindled before the king. She turned her face to Cathmor, from amidst her waving locks. 'Sooner shall the eagle of heaven be torn from the stream of his roaring wind, when he sees the dun prey before him, the young sons of the bounding roe, than thou, O Cathmor, be turned from the strife of renown. Soon may I see thee, warrior, from the skirts of the evening mist, when it is rolled around me, on Lona of the streams. While yet thou art distant far, strike, Cathmor, strike the shield, that joy may return to my darkened soul, as I lean on the mossy rock. But if thou shouldst fall, I am in the land of strangers; O send thy voice, from thy cloud, to the maid of Inis-huna!' (Temora Book VIII in *The Poems of Ossian,* translated by James Macpherson Esq., London 1819, p. 456).

Macpherson uses the stock vocabulary of minor eighteenth-century poetry and tries to achieve an effect of "primitivism" by making the sentence structure as unrhythmical as possible, and the sense structure as incoherent as possible. It simply reads like a bad translation - which was, after all, more or less Macpherson's intention.

18 The description of Gamut's funeral hymn has already been quoted

earlier in this essay.

19 *The Wing and Wing,* Leatherstocking edition, London n.d., Chapter IV p. 54 (italics mine). Faulkner, in *Knight's Gambit,* refers to his four main characters as being "like the stock characters in the slick magazine serial." The device has a respectable lineage: it certainly goes back as far as the Chorus to *Henry V* and to Macbeth's "poor player that struts and frets his hour upon the stage."

20 See John Speirs, *Poetry twoards Novel* (London, 1971).

WRITING NEW ENGLANDY: A STUDY OF DICTION AND TECHNIQUE IN THE POETRY OF EMILY DICKINSON

In spite of recent attempts to trivialize the life and work of Emily Dickinson her place in American letters is surely secure. The uncertain path to mature evaluation, one which still appears to be required of most nineteenth-century American artists, has been completed, and finally we are in a position to evaluate her work in the critical tranquillity necessary without feeling compelled to defend our object of study. Though her position may be secure in this general way, clearly a host of problems remains, the most significant of which continues to be that of her specific place in the intellectual climate of the last century. Is she merely a rather pessimistic Transcendentalist, one who chose, with Melville and Hawthorne, to affirm the shadows in the bright picture presented by Emerson? Or is she the last passionate Puritan, a daughter of Jonathan Edwards, who in the death rattle of that noble failure found the tones of her most remarkable contemporaries, Kierkegaard and Nietzsche?

To be sure, no literary critic wants this alternative forced upon him though a cursory glance over the criticism of the past twenty years reveals that most critics have, consciously or unconsciously, chosen a particular role for Miss Dickinson. But once such loyalties have been declared, the poetry suffers, for it is placed in a framework which it was certainly never meant to bear and the delicacy of the verse, particularly its impish humor, is completely lost. That is to say, Emily Dickinson becomes a vaguely unbelieving post-Emersonian Transcendentalist, while in the specific commentary upon her work we find the rhetoric of modern American eschatological despair projected into the detail of her poetry. Thus, the critical base for true criticism is sundered, for the critic, after desultory attention to her nineteenth-century background, now feels free to use the poet as an eloquent spokesman for our present discontents.

There is, as far as I can determine, only one way out of this profound confusion and lack of clarity, and that is to begin by placing the poet firmly and securely in her rather remarkable family and home town. In other words, we still need a detailed study of the Dickinsons in Amherst as well as a similar investigation into the peculiar life of the Connecticut River Valley in the first half of the last century. On the basis of such studies the detail of the poet's language as well as the specific thrust of her thinking could be laid bare in such a way that the precise value of her poetry would be revealed. In *The Life of Emily Dickinson* R.B. Sewall has undertaken to present in the first volume of his study, the poet's family background in greater detail than heretofore has been attempted in order "to broaden the factual context against which any theoretical interpretation might be measured."[1] In his second volume Sewall proceeds to discuss "her sense of the mystery of things. Central to this mystery ... was the mystery of herself" (p. 5). And he is forced to conclude that "Emily Dickinson cut no figure at all, but in a deeper sense her life was figurative, metaphoric" (p. 11).

The importance of Sewall's work to the critic of Miss Dickinson's poetry is difficult to underestimate. He has broadened and deepened "the factual context" by bringing together and synthesizing the findings of all the more important scholars in the field since Johnson. The turbulent lives of the three Dickinson children are now much more clear, for the work of Leyda, Todd, Anderson and others has now been brought together in such a way that the 'mist' at the centre, the poet herself, is almost revealed. By careful study most of the speculation about her unhappy love affair has been answered as well as the so-called 'mystery' surrounding her withdrawalfrom society. And what remains, to be sure, is as simple and as mysterious as ever, the genius of the poetry.

Although we agree that, together with Walt Whitman, Emily Dickinson is the most important poet of the last century, why, having said that, does a nagging doubt still remain with regard to her achievement as a poet? Surely, Ivor Winters does not cast so long a shadow! Surely, at this late date the length of her individual poems has no effect upon our judgment, and neither does her often eccentric use of language. Nonetheless, the critic Robert Weisbuch, in his *Emily Dickinson's Poetry,* finds it necessary to escape her insistent brevity by feeling compelled "to view Dickinson's lyrics as one long poem, to the same extent that Whitman's lyrics constitute a *Leaves of Grass*."[2] According to Weisbuch, therefore, the critic of Miss Dickinson must "search for the underlying characteristics which unite the poems" (p. XIII).

Indeed, all literary critics must begin where they are, with the presuppositions made inevitable by the qualities of their private sensibilities, and any urgent specification of that critical foundation will of necessity be prejudicial to further literary judgments. To assume that there is a monolithic unity beneath this poetry is, in the first and most obvious instance, to fly in the face of the facts, namely, that there is no evidence to suggest that such a unity ever existed. Furthermore, it is to assume that either all the poetry was written by the same person, or that it all possesses the same underlying significance. And the latter is as dangerous as the former is foolish. The critic is certainly free to find the brevity of Miss Dickinson's poetry unfortunate, but unless he can show that there is a special monotony about them, one which no one hitherto has discovered, the individual poems ought to be read individually, for themselves alone. Then after a concensus has been revealed, the common imagery and theme may be discussed with justification.

But Weisbuch might indignantly reply to this by saying, I have not pushed a specific theme onto her poetry; rather, I have sought out the basic metaphysical stance beneath it. He could then continue, as he does, to assert that "Dickinson develops her meanings by a peculiarly overt and furious process of analogy-making ... In short, what I'm after is a compound vision of the compounder herself" (p. XII). To which one ought certainly to reply, but just what is the nature of this "analogy-making." And what, to continue, makes it so terribly distinctive in the work of this particular poet that it should be found so uniquely characteristic of her approach to the craft of poetry?

In spite of many incidental critical successes in *Emily Dickinson's Poetry* the argument of the book as a whole is committed to a series of fundamental methodological presuppositions that are simply unable to bear the weight of the argument placed upon them. According to Weisbuch the essence of Miss Dickinson's poetic method is analogy, and to him "analogy becomes a way of poetic life" (p.12). To continue, her typical poem "enacts a hypothesis about the world by patterning a parallel, analogical world" (p. 12). Therefore, she may be called an "analogical poet because analogy suggests an extended equation (*a* is to *b* as *c* is to *d*) carried out by a rigorous logic whose comparisons are always functional and never merely decorative" (p. 13).

Insofar as this is not all completely tautological, the inescapable question is, of course, what does Weisbuch mean by *analogy?* And how does it differ from the more customary ideas of metaphor and symbol? Unfortunately, I cannot escape the impression that the critic has indulged himself in that most dangerous American habit of having borrowed a term from another, highly sophisticated discipline without really taking the trouble to discover just what that term actually means. For there is probably no more difficult notion in the history of philosophical theology than that of analogy. Without going in too great detail, it ought to be mentioned that there are at least three kinds of analogy which exist in a scale of progression running from univocity to complete symbolism, and further, that the one noted above in the over-simplified form of a mathematical proportion is the *analogia entis,* the only form adequate enough, according to Aquinas and Suarez, to indicate the relation between God and His creation. The major difficulty with any application of this sort of analogy is that the two major terms of the equation, God and the world, differ so very greatly that any comparison is hardly more than a metaphysical compliment unless it has first been informed by the lesser, more univocal kinds of analogy, those which assert a more positive connection between the Divine and the created.

In the first place, then, it is difficult to see how a consistent application of such an idea could ever help us understand a poem, and it is sufficient evidence of the failure of this method that with all the extremely helpful criticism Weisbuch's work contains, none of it is dependent in any way on the use of the *analogy entis*. But in spite of this manifest failure Weisbuch has raised the serious question of the status of much of Miss Dickinson's diction, and it is apparent from many of her poems as well as many of her letters that she is palying with the language in a way which, I believe, continues to evade most of her critics. In spite of many-studies dealing with the various sources of her vocabulary, and in spite of the presence of a very complete and unusually helpful concordance to her poetry, much of that poetry seems willfully obscure, almost as though the poet were doing her best, not only to fool us, but to go so far as to suggest a world of meanings which are meant to be closed to us forever.[3]

At this point in the argument it seems appropriate to take a step backwards and review the situation from a slightly different perspective while bearing two basic facts in mind. First of all, the poet grew up in a part of New England with a very special religious history in which Solomon Stoddard and Jonathan Edwards played remarkable roles. The Connecticut River Valley was noted for its allegiance to a particularly earnest kind of American Calvinism in which the place of the word and the Word had a peculiar significance. And in the second place, Miss Dickinson refused from her very early years to participate in the religious life of her family and of the community in the ways expected of her. In other words, she was the inheritor of a particular tradition to which she was unable to give her complete and total loyalties. And this made it possible for her to use that tradition, and especially its verbal aspect, with the impishness for which she is renowned.

Readers of Miss Dickinson's early letters have noted that in her correspondence with her one-time schoolmate, Abdiah Root, she often uses words, long phrases and even complete sentences which reflect very special religious circumstances and, hence, meanings, most of which seem to have been a reaction to Miss Dickinson's inability to participate in a religious revival at Mt. Holyoke. Of particular interest in this regard is the letter of the 31st January, 1846, in which the poet reveals the religious condition which was to be hers throughout her life:

> I was almost persuaded to be a christian. I thought I never again could be thoughtless and worldly - and I can say that I never emjoyed such perfect peace and happiness as the short time in which I felt I had found my saviour. But I soon forgot my morning prayer or else it was irksome to me. One by one my old habits returned and I cared less for religion than ever. I have longed to hear from you - to know what decision you have made. I hope you are a christian for I feel that it is impossible for any one to be happy without a treasure in heaven. I feel that I shall never be happy without I love Christ.[4]

And she continues: "I am far from thoughtless upon the subject of religion. I continually hear Christ saying to me Daughter give me thine heart." Later, she continues with what was to become one of her most compelling ideas: "Does not Eternity appear dreadful to you. I often get thinking of it and it seems so dark to me that I almost wish there was no Eternity."

The important thing about the passages quoted above is not only the obvious religious concern of the young Miss Dickinson, but also the words and phrases which she uses to convey that concern. And anyone who was raised in American Fundamentalist orthodoxy will undoubtedly recognize some of them as being current even today. For it is not simply a matter of using *Christ* but of saying *I shall never be happy without I love Christ,* and His own admonition to Miss Dickinson, *Daughter give me thine heart*. Throughout the letters we continue to find this kind of use of religious language, sometimes she mocks and disparages ideas that do not appeal to her, while at others she expresses a certain homesickness for the older securities. One thing is certain, however, the language is very much her own.

Although the diction of personal correspondence may have only a slight and tenuous relation to a poet's use of language in his or her verse, it is important to recall at this point that Emily Dickinson has often been appropriated as a religious poet. Her famous poem, "I never saw a Moor -" (1052)[5] has been anthologised so very often by religious people in their publications that it has almost become a commonplace among the orthodox in America, even though she also wrote a poem as devastating to the Christian faith as "He strained my faith-" (497), to take a single, striking example from among many.

The temptation at this point is, quite obviously, to turn our attention to the content of the poetry and to analyze it theologically. Such a strategy, however, would inevitably take us away from the poetry itself, so that it is more appropriate to study a particular poem and see if it is possible to discover something about her poetic technique. Consider, for example, the following:

> "Faith" is a fine invention
> When Gentlemen can *see* -
> But *Microscopes* are prudent
> In an emergency. (185)

The word *faith* immediately calls to mind "faith, hope and charity" as well as "the shield of faith" and "by grace are ye saved through faith," not forgetting the opening to the eleventh chapter of the Epistle to the Hebrews, "Now faith is the substance of things hoped for, the evidence of things not seen."

The poem, to the contrary, asserts that *faith* is an *invention* in an age remarkable for inventions. It is man-made and hardly the gift of God her church and her believing family and friends certainly held that it was. Furthermore, it would appear to be the special possession of "Gentlemen" who can *"see,"* and one can well imagine the young doubter before the elders and deacons of the First Church who probably affirmed that this faith was very much in their possession. And the fact that she turns, as she usually does in instances such as this one, to this very physical world, the world brought close by microscopes with such urgency, indicates all the more surely her inability to share the faith of her fathers completely.

From a more literary perspective it is obvious that the success of this little poem depends upon the echo of the passage from Hebrews. By asserting such a bold contrast to that well-known passage, the poet urges her own message upon the reader with all the greater emphasis. No "substance of things not seen" but the world aided, enhanced, even accented with the aid of a microscope. Furthermore, one needs this terribly physical encouragement at just that point where the believer is most likely to rely upon his faith, "in an emergency." Miss Dickinson's systematic misuse of religious language could hardly be better illustrated, by disappointing the expectations of her readers in this unique way, she has made herself all the more clear.

The poet uses this technique so often that it is very clear that she knew precisely what she was about. To take another example, her several games with the word *hope* are quite remarkable. Although this word appears in the Bible so often that it is impossible to give even an introductory impression of its meaning here, its place in 1st Corinthians 13 has already been noted above, while it also appears in well-known passages in Colossians and 1st Thessalonians. Its presence in the passage from Hebrews is also of importance here. In the fifth verse of the first chapter of Colossians the Apostle speaks of "the hope which is laid up for you in heaven," and in the twenty-third verse of the same chapter he talks of believers who are "not moved away from the hope of the gospel." In Titus 2:13 we read, "looking for that blessed hope, and glorious appearing of the great God and our Saviour Jesus Christ." In 1st Thessalonians Paul speaks of "the hope of salvation," (5:13) while we must not forget "the substance of things hoped for."

In the poetry there are three short poems about the subject which immediately attract the attention, "Hope is the thing with feathers-" (254), "Hope is a strange invention-" (1392) and "Hope is a subtle Glutton-" (1547). Written, if we follow Johnson's tentative though convincing method of dating, in 1861, 1877 and 1882 respectively, these poems reflect in the opening lines the same technique as was used in the poem of faith. These openings are clearly meant to surprise, even to shock perhaps, the reader, for in each instance the *hope* offered is certainly not the one expected. One does not, in Christian terms at least, think of hope as a "thing with feathers," something barely a bird in the first instance, for in the opening stanza it has been remarkably denaturalized. In fact, one almost gets the feeling that there is something automatic, mindless about its singing. To be sure, in the following stanza it is obvious that hope does function effectively for many people in time of need, "the little Bird/that kept so many warm" (11. 7-8). But in spite of its positive work for others, it has never "asked a crumb - of Me" (1. 12). The poet remains strangely distant, unacquainted with the works of this second Christian virtue.

In the second poem on hope mechanical, or better the language of nineteenth-century technology prevails, to an even greater degree than in the poem on faith discussed above. In the first stanza it is suggested that hope is a kind of *perpetuum mobile,* a patented invention in that era of technological proliferation, working in the heart, never wearing out. In the second and last stanza hope is made "electric" and its "momentum" is claimed to "Embellish all we own-" (1. 8). In such a brief compass the yearning mystery of the Faith has been reduced in a very systematic way to something that is manifestly alien to the personal core of a picture of the future.

In the last of the three poems this virtue is called a "subtle Glutton" (1.1) who, remarkably, "feeds upon the Fair -" (1.1). And though this glutton continues to gorge himself, the same amount of food remains before him so that he can go on eating. Leaving to one side the whole question of the beliefs of Emily Dickinson herself, interesting though they may be, it seems clear to me that the effectiveness of this and the other poems depends upon the fact the reader Miss Dickinson had in mind was to have certain expectations clothed in specific semantic structures, the commonplaces of a special form of Calvinism that had been realized over two hundred years in a specific community. And the meaning of the poems, their very success in capturing the imagination, depends now upon our ability to appreciate this verbally aggressive stance in relation to the primary context out of which it came.[6]

In another poem, one no longer using the language of the local church so rigidly, Miss Dickinson extends this technique to one of the basic practices of the believer.

Prayer is the little implement
Through which Men reach
Where Presence - is denied them.
They fling their Speech

By means of it - in God's Ear -
If then He hear -
This sums the Apparatus
Comprised in Prayer - (437)

Here, once again, the mechanical is suggested by "implement" and "apparatus," and this certainly has implications for the poet's view of the practice. One notices, too, the strange attitude of those who pray, "flinging" their supplications at God, perhaps in anger, more probably in haste and nonchalance. But it is equally important to note that there is no assurance that God will hear, let alone answer that which has been thrown at Him. Once again, it is manifest that the success of the poem depends upon defeating expectations, but in this case those expectations are no longer verbal as before but are based upon a general religious practice about which the poet entertains most serious doubts. The technique, then, is no longer a linguistic one and can now easily be extended into any area of custom or habit, so that it may be seen as a particular example of the general notion of defeated expectations.

Were this technique not representative for the work of the poet, were it only an occasional trick or aberration in an otherwise quite different *oevre*, the foregoing would be most incidental to an understanding of Emily Dickinson's poetry. Further investigation reveals, however, that her systematic use of similar trickery lies at the heart of some of her more important poems, especially those dealing with God, Heaven and immortality. Miss Dickinson's notion of God has been much discussed, and her strange heterodoxy, it has been claimed, is based primarily upon her own experience of her own father. (Indeed, it would be surprising were it otherwise.) Although Mr.Dickinson undoubtedly played the most significant role in the formation of this basic metaphor, that metaphor is now, after all, clothed in the structures of the verse where it no longer functions as the head of a family but rather as the substance of several, somewhat discordant meanings. And these meanings are remarkably varied, and although they reveal little growth or development during the course of the poet's life, they run the spectrum from orthodoxy to heterodoxy with striking alacrity.[7]

After five other substantives, the word *God* is the most frequent in the poetry, appearing 130 times.[8] Among those other five it is interesting to note that *Heaven* is to be found 143 times, while on 141 occasions she uses *Death*. Given the habitual brevity of the verse this reveals a truly significant religious preoccupation, and one is sorely tempted to enter into the theological lists at this point. But our interest lies with the peculiar way in which the poetry deals with this notion. And in an early poem we read:

I never lost as much but twice,
And that was in the sod.
Twice have I stood a beggar
Before the door of God!

Angels - twice descending
Reimbursed my store -
Burglar! Banker - Father!
I am poor once more! (49)

Although biographers may continue to speculate about the occasion of this poem, its general meaning is quite clear. The poet, hurt deeply twice by the deaths of dear ones, found divine solace on those two previous occasions, but the third bereavement threatens to be inconsolable, and the poet in her anger and despair calls God, "Burglar! Banker - Father!" (1.7) The line ought to be read so that its two meanings, two meanings that reinforce one another here and do not constitute ambiguity, remain clear and firm. On the one hand, the line can be read to mean that after the dash, or pause, the speaker acquiesces to the will of God and once again accepts Him as Father. Read this way, she affirms anew, not my will, but Thy Will be done. On the other hand, the line can be read heavy with irony: you are a burglar, one who has stolen from me; a banker, one who keeps accounts and judges that three is too many; notwithstanding, you maintain that you are my father! In both readings the significance of the line is built up in a double way, both refinements of the technique outlined above. Firstly, the notion that God is a thief and bookkeeper in the context of mourning is certainly shocking enough. And then, secondly, he remains "father," with all the religious associations that word continues to have, while this meaning refers back to the claim that he is also a burglar and a banker. Thus, in an extremely simple line, the poet has achieved such technical mastery of her language that she is able to say more about the irrationality of death than many theologians have been able to say in complete books.

Were this the only example of such heterodoxy, it might be taken as an exception to an otherwise orthodox rule, but that is far from being the case. Perhaps, there is no word in religious usage more tied to specific, approved linguistic structures that the word *God,* but that does not keep Miss Dickinson from being light and frivolous and wonder in one of her lesser verses what kind of heaven the "Papa above" has prepared for the mice in her kitchen (61). So, too, she can also wonder, more seriously this time, why God has hidden heaven so carefully (191), and though He may be our "old Neighbour" (623), a statement without any real surprises, He is also called "that Bold Person, God" (900), a truly "Awful Father of Love" (1204). In a similar way He is accused of being a physician who is always too late with his cure and in the same poem an exchequer making demands (1270), while in another well-known poem He is called "a Mighty Merchant, one who sneered" (621). And when the poet has a strange and unpleasant vision of heaven, God is a necromancer as well as a landlord (115), while when he has failed to answer prayer, he is simply a "Swindler" (476). Her view of God in this regard is uncompromising:

> Of Course - I prayed -
> And did God Care? (376)

The effectiveness of these startling descriptions of the virtues of God depends, almost always on the way in which she disturbs the usual meaning of the word. When she becomes more precise by giving her statements a firmer, more specific frame, her remarks can become truly shocking, they certainly must have been in her time and place. In a poem which talks of a "King" and his orchard, she concludes:

> And I omit to pray
> "Father, thy will be done" today
> For my will goes the other way,
> And it were perjury! (103)

In another poem she threatens God with a law suit because he took, among other things, her garden (116). And she affirms aggressively at one point:

> Whether Deity's guiltless
> My business is, to find. (178)

For:

> "Heavenly Father" - take to thee
> The supreme iniquity
> Fashioned by thy candid Hand
> In a moment contraband -
> Though to trust us - seem to us
> More respectful - "We are Dust" -
> We apologize to thee
> For thine own Duplicity - (1461)

The poet's treatment of this word, however, may be most clearly seen in her treatment of the notion that God's eye is on the sparrow to which one might add the Parable of the Ninety and Nine. Not only are "Sparrows, unnoticed by the Father - /Lambs for whom time had not a fold" (141), but "Mama never forgets her birds" (164), in fact, she cares for them properly. Indeed, "God gave a Loaf to every Bird - / But just a Crumb - to Me -" (791). After all, we are expected to ask God's forgiveness for an unknown crime (1601), and though we are as children before Him, a stance the poet often assumes, nonetheless:

Far from Love the Heavenly Father
Leads the Chosen Child,
Oftener through Realm of Briar
Than the Meadow mild.

Oftener by the Claw of Dragon
Than the Hand of Friend
Guides the Little One predestined
To the Native Land. (1021)

Because the content of much of this poetry is not at all strange to post-Christian man, it is relatively easy to underestimate just what is going on here. The poet never really says that God does not exist, but she does ask with great earnestness what kind of a God he really is. "I know that He exists" is the opening line of one of her poems (33), but she continues as follows:

Somewhere - in Silence -
He has hid his rare life
From our gross eyes.

'Tis an instant's play
'Tis a fond Ambush -
Just to make Bliss
Earn her own Surprise!

But - should the play
Prove piercing earnest -
Should the glee - glaze -
In Death's - stiff - stare -

Would not the fun
Look too expensive!
Would not the jest -
Have crawled too far!

In the universe of this conclusion is atheism the easy option.

As the reader has no doubt noticed, perhaps with no little irritation, it has been most difficult not to discuss Emily Dickinson's religion in the preceding argument, and it may have been unrealistic to have tried, however unsuccessfully, to do so. Yet the method has been fruitful if it has isolated a technique in Miss Dickinson's poetry when, confronting the world of cliché and commonplace in Amherst, she attempted to say something uniquely her own. She did so, not as many have suggested by using particular words as though they were the atoms of meaning which were ready to be fixed in the molecules of the poems. No, she began with the well-known phrases and sentences and parables of the life around her and twisted them in such a shocking way that, by calculating the surprise, they could reveal her special meanings. For in the last analysis she knew as well as any professional theologians that:

Embarrassment of one another
And God
Is Revelation's limit,
Aloud
Is nothing that is chief
But still,
Divinity dwells under seal. (662)

Free University, Amsterdam August J. Fry

NOTES

1 R.B. Sewall, *The Life of Emily Dickinson* (London: Faber & Faber, Two Volumes, 1974 and 1976, respectively), p. 4 (Vol. I). Further page references are to this edition.
2 Robert Weisbuch, *Emily Dickinson's Poetry* (Chicago: The University of Chicago Press, 1975), p. XIII. Further page references are to this edition.
3 The preceding argument is found, in a much briefer form, in my review "A Critical Bibliography of American Literature to 1900" in DQR, vol. 8, 1979/ 1, 54-57.
4 *The Letters of Emily Dickinson,* ed. Thomas H. Johnson (Cambridge: Harvard University Press, 1958, vol. 1, no. 10), p. 27f. The difference in tone and vocabulary between the letters written to Miss Root and those written to other correspondents is truly remarkable.
5 Texts and numbering of Miss Dickinson's poems have been taken from the three-volume Variorum edition of her poetry, ed. Thomas H. Johnson, Cambridge: Harvard University Press, 1955.
6 For a significant complement to this argument, see Suzanne M. Wilson, "Structural Patterns in the Poetry of Emily Dickinson," *American Literature,* XXXV, (1963-64), 53-59.
7 Compare Nina Baym, "God, Father, and Lover in Emily Dickinson's Poetry," in *Puritan Influences in American Literature,* ed. by Emory Elliot (Urbana: University of Illinois Press, 1979) pp. 193-209.
8 In the appendix to *A Concordance to the Poems of Emily Dickinson,* ed. S.P. Rosenbaum (Ithaca: Cornell University Press, 1964), p. 865. Although this is a most useful book, its basic approach to the poetry is very much at odds with my argument.

A COMPLETE IMAGE: JAMES'S *THE BOSTONIANS*

While I have the greatest difficulty in disagreeing with anything T.A. Birrell has to say about *The Bostonians* in his excellent article published a few years back,[1] there are certain matters arising out of that article that I would like to elaborate on, and one or two other matters that seem worth going into. My own aims will be fairly limited, in comparison with the broad critical sweep of that article, and the clear and scholarly placing of *The Bostonians* in a large (yet particular and significant) context, that Birrell gives us. I shall concentrate more on interpretation in a fairly narrow sense, not because I favour that brand of all too common literary activity which these days makes do for both criticism and scholarship, but because I begin to believe that almost anything one can do to make an academic or non-academic public enjoy Henry James must be done. My own experience is that even students of literature are less alive to him to-day than ten or fifteen years ago. Maybe he will never be a popular novelist outside Utopia (and which of the great novelists is in any significant sense popular anywhere else?), but he ought to be more read and enjoyed if nowhere else then at least within the confines of a university. So one of my main concerns is to ask not so much the large question about his general lack of popularity (there must be a lot of truth in the common verdict that ascribes this to his close analytical method, the difficulty of his language, even his obscurity, etc., arguments which are often simply pejorative ways of indicating his intelligence); no, all that I would like to start with is asking why *The Bostonians* is not readily acknowledged as one of the great novels? Why this of all things?

The fact that one finds *The Bostonians* a really great work of art implies, no doubt, something about one's own view of literature, and there are always those who would like one to define this. "What is a great novel?" a colleague asked recently in public, exasperated at everyone's inability to give a definition. But the definition, in literature, if it is to be worth anything, must almost inevitably be tied rather tightly to a particular. I fear in the present instance I shall not have space for defining even why *The Bostonians* is a great novel, never mind about my "view of literature."

One has the feeling that prejudices are, and perhaps have always been, somewhat rampant in relation to James, which is why, in defending him, one feels obliged to be more than usually explicit, must risk maintaining the obvious. Particularly when one comes to see how some of the best arguments fail to persuade. When Birrell states that what James is really saying in this novel is that "he who generalizes is an ass" (p. 250),[2] and when he argues that "the novel does not pose any question of whether Verena should or whether she shouldn't" (p. 254) surrender to Basil Ransom - and these are things that must be said and needed saying - one is not very confident that these are going to be very persuasive affirmations to those who see the book as in some sense a statement by James on the feminist movement, or to those who in a somewhat similar way see it as a document of the History of Ideas in the 19th century. But they must at all events be answered, for though their verdicts on the novel may not be hostile, they can well be misleading.

Elizabeth Schultz[3] sees the movement led by Olive Chancellor as an evil force which the good hero opposes (it is with a certain relief that one notices this author was not a man); and Theodore C. Miller[4] sees James here turning conservative and attacking the *liberal* Olive Chancellor in this novel. It is not that I am trying to hold this sort of comment up to ridicule. There is a very evident polarization going on within the novel. Even Kenneth Graham can assert, in his discussion of *The Tragic Muse,* that it is "less black and white than *The Bostonians",*[5] though he does not specify, who is black and who is white. It might seem too obvious to specify, but not in the light of the articles mentioned above in this paragraph.

The fact of the matter is that during one's reading of *The Bostonians* one is perpetually aware of the Feminists and their Cause. One might say that it is a hardy (or perhaps even cynical) reader who can remain entirely untouched throughout, or undistracted, by a sense of a certain unfairness inherent in the position of women. Though an irritation with the "Cause" seems also a justifiable reaction. At all events the reader is liable to be provoked. James is dealing with a material that rouses and inflames passions and prejudices in a multiple of unforeseen ways. It is a public issue where feelings run high now as ever, so that one need not altogether be surprised at this undue tendency to take sides, and to see it in black and white terms. To take one example: Verena, in her speech at Mrs Burrage's on the position of women, ends on this note:

> Some of you say that we have already all the influence we can possibly require, and talk as if we ought to be grateful that we are allowed even to breathe. Pray, who shall judge what we require if not we ourselves? We require simple freedom; we require the lid to be taken off the box in which we have been kept for centuries. You say it's a very comfortable, cosy, convenient box, with nice glass sides, so that we can see out, and all that's wanted is to give another quiet turn to the key. That is very easily answered. Good gentlemen, you have never been in the box, and you haven't the least idea how it feels.[6]

In the first place what seems so wonderful here is the developed Verena manner - the gentle and friendly placidity in which the embarrassing moral challenge is couched (the irony is that she is in Olive's "box," and it is Ransom who is going to give her, as we shall see a sense of freedom). It is no doubt a naive statement, but it is naive in the way some leaders of resistance or liberation movements are naive - where the naiveté is not the most important aspect of what they are saying. The trained reader may suspect the whole motivation behind such a use of language, but his suspicion need not be more than a means for escaping the raw problem - on the grounds that the sentiments expressed are not sophisticatedly or delicately enough conceived. If one takes this speech as simply exemplifying the kindly artlessness and well-learnt lesson of Verena Tarrant, is one not cynically blinding oneself to the very serious issue she raises about the position of women? My immediate answer would be - No, one is not cynically blinding oneself. But it is essential to ask the question because it seems very likely that many readers do and will take James to be examining the feminist movement and the position of women, whereas he is in fact examining personal motivation and the corrupting effect of abstract causes on individuals, as Birrell says. I would even add that James has gone to great lengths to ensure that while the novel is *not* to be taken as a comment on women's rights *per se,* it is most certainly intimated that the Feminist Cause is as liable as many another to have a corrupting effect on its leaders and members - and there may well be readers who will not like recognizing this.

Again one might ask whether James did not blunder in selecting material that could be so liable to rouse passions and prejudices, that could so easily distract the reader from attending with precision to what he, James, is saying and doing? Does he not supply strong stimuli to irrelevant response (to use an old and tried I.A. Richard's term), which give rise to misleading discussions on the merits of the novel? Well, if the material is explosive, it is all the more challenging to the artist and gripping for the reader - and it should be fairly demonstrable that James managed admirably. One could start by saying that the feminist cause is a background issue to the real conflict. It is something exploited by Olive to justify her obsessive interest in Verena. And it is an issue that is 'placed' (that is, in relation to the action of this novel) by Miss Birdseye and Dr Prance. It is a cause that has a martyr - in Miss Birdseye - a comic and at the same time tragic martyr. She illustrates symbolically the weakness of committing oneself to an abstraction; yet she has the appeal of a kind of loving commitment to humanity. At the other extreme there is Dr Prance, another comic symbol, but this time of the *really* emancipated woman. When Ransom (who likes her) asks her about "Mrs Farrinder's system," Dr Prance replies: "Well, what it amounts to is just that women want to have a better time. That's what it comes to in the end. I am aware of that, without her telling me." "And don't you sympathise with such an aspiration?" (asks Ransom) "Well, I don't know as I cultivate the sentimental side," said Doctor Prance. "There's plenty of sympathy without mine. If they want to have a better time, I suppose it's natural; so do men too, I suppose. But I don't know as it appeals to me - to make sacrifices for it; it ain't such a wonderful time - the best you *can* have!" (pp. 37-38). Prance is independent, tough, emancipated, and she cares. She cares for her patients, she cares for Miss Birdseye. Ransom respects her. If the Movement collapses she will survive, a woman with a vocation. If she embodies a criticism of the Movement, she also embodies a way out. James is not exploring the movement, but it would not be James if he did not give us a number of points of view the better to see the whole matter in perspective. It is the fairest method you can devise, and it is the novelist's method above all. And as Birrell points out, not the philosopher's (p. 250). James does not shirk comment, does not refrain from giving us something of the reality of the feminist movement, but what he is doing is exploring something much more important and much less popular, viz. the subtle and urgent workings of human love and fear, loyalty, treachery and hypocrisy, embodied in particular characters in dramatic situations. The central conflict between Basil Ransom and Olive Chancellor is a personal issue, a personal quarrel. It is for the possession of Verena as a desired object that they *both* fight. Their political affiliations significantly intensify their feelings of hostility for each other - and that is the dramatic function of these affiliations. Most discussion of the 'politics' of the novel can be called misinterpretation if it misses this crucial point. The 'politics,' the affiliations, exist for James primarily in the resultant effects on individual psyches, if you like.

He gives us a useful clue on the second page of his novel: "The Reader," he writes, "who likes a complete image, who desires to read with the senses as well as with the reason, is entreated not to forget" of Basil Ransom "that he prolonged his consonants and swallowed his vowels..." The complete image of Basil Ransom is something very much richer than what can be distilled from his being a Southern gentleman and his disliking the feminist cause, just as Olive is not to be defined merely in terms of her membership of this cause, or Verena either, for that matter. Without their very particular bents and qualities there could have been no clash at all. Without his nerve *and* tenderness Ransom would never, one imagines, have won Verena; and without his harsh opposition to the women's movement and his overpowering masculinity, Olive would not have fought him off so desperately. There were other men she did not object to. One could say that the novel is a political or ideological document only if one leaves 'the complete image' out of the account, only if one fails to read with the senses as well as with the reason. If it is argued that Olive is single-mindedly idealistic, that for her everything is subservient to the ends of the Movement (even to the extent of her being willing to buy Verena from her parents and sell her to Mrs Burrage!), one cannot deny that an obsessive desire to possess Verena complicates her whole motivation. Even Verena recognizes this:

> When she felt her trembling that way before luncheon it made her [Verena] quite sick to realize how much her friend was wrapped up in her - how terribly she would suffer from the least deviation (p. 252).

The intensity of the purely personal involvement *must* prevent one from taking her motivation as primarily ideological. (If this is a very obvious argument, it is all the more strange that the novel should ever be looked upon as presenting an ideological clash.)

It is not Olive's image, then, that is lacking in Jamesian completeness. But I have heard objections to the alleged 'imbecility' of Verena. Maybe these need not be taken very seriously, yet it does seem to me that it is in the character of Verena that our imaginations are most challenged to recognize something that could be called completeness. It would be worth looking at her more closely.

To use Blake's terms again - and they are often apt for the novel in the 19th century - Ransom is Experience,[7] Verena is Innocence - and she remains innocent throughout in spite of her learning to conceal things, from Olive for instance (for Blake, of course, concealing things is very much a symptom of experience). And she remains innocent in spite of the fact that she discovers - and she is "aghast" at it - that her conviction of "responsive friendship" for Olive and of "pity for the sufferings of women in general" could crumble "into colourless dust ... in three short months" (p. 332). She is innocent because she follows the natural dictates of her feelings throughout:

> she was not ashamed of the treachery which she - yes, decidedly, by this time she must admit to herself - she meditated. It was simply that the trust had changed sides; that radiant image began to look at her from Basil Ransom's expressive eyes (p. 332).

And because she is true to her feelings and at the same time very sensitive to the feelings of others, one recognizes the truth of Ransom's biased verdict that she is "quite incorruptible" and "above all vulgarizing influences" (p. 292).

Yet to see Verena as inane or imbecile is not altogether to miss the point. Early in the novel when, at Olive's house, Ransom is pleased to find that Verena smiles at him we are indeed told that he "could not know that this was fatuous, that she smiled so at everyone" (p. 77). Further on we read:

> She took all that was given her and was grateful, and missed nothing that was withheld; she was the most extraordinary mixture of eagerness and docility (p. 93).

A hundred pages further we have her telling Ransom that Olive makes her speeches

> "or the best part of them. She tells me what to say - the real things, the strong things. It's Miss Chancellor as much as me!" said the singular girl, with a generous complacency which was yet half ludicrous (p. 194).

There is certainly something of the parrot in her. But these qualities - and she certainly has them - are qualities that attend on innocence, and in her case convey her essential individuality. She is representatively innocent, but not an ideal or an absolute or a symbol of anything. Her approval of "free unions" (p. 106) is comically unconventional but in character. James has risked making her fatuous because he has the creative power to make her that and so much more.

> She had no worldly pride, no traditions of independence, no ideas of what was done and what was not done (p. 150).

The comment is implicitly Olive's, but is none the less convincing for that reason, and being phrased negatively is all the more suggestive both of the inadequacy of her upbringing (her *tabula rasa* is strikingly blank), and of the naturalness of her child-like development. "The blood of the lecture-going, night-walking Tarrants did distinctly flow in her veins" (p. 255), but it has not been tainted; it is fresh and natural. She has the irresponsible fantasy of a child at times, as her first response to Mrs Luna shows, where she thinks "that if she could have chosen at the beginning she would have liked to resemble Mrs Luna. This lady fascinated her, carried off her imagination to strange lands" (pp. 94-95). Strange lands where she is free to imagine. The walk she takes with Ransom in the Central Park is just such a strange excursion to her eager imagination:

> Once Verena was fairly launched the spirit of the day took possession of her; she was glad to have come, she forgot about Olive, enjoyed the sense of wandering in the great city with a remarkable young man who would take beautiful care of her, while no one else in the world knew where she was. It was very different from her drive yesterday with Mr Burrage, but it was more free, more intense, more full of amusing incident and opportunity (p. 282).

This freedom ("no one else in the world knew where she was") is just what she does not feel with Olive. As was pointed out earlier, she is in Olive's "box." Put differently - "her whole relation to Olive was one of tacit, tender assent to passionate insistence" (p. 285), and on the same page - "it was in her nature to be easily submissive." It is this, along with her kindly consideration, that keeps her tied to Olive, while it is her "power of enjoyment" (p. 246), which Olive rightly fears, that pulls her towards Ransom (not that we are given to understand that her ultimate "freedom" with Ransom will always be of the kind she enjoyed in the Central Park.

It does not seem necessary to follow through to the end of the various developments in Verena's relationships with the other two main characters. The necessary points have mostly, I hope, been made. It has been argued that her innocence lies chiefly in her obeying the dictates of feeling - and certainly in the later stages her innocence, naturalness and consideration for others are put thoroughly to the test. But James has been so lucid and precise, so creatively complete, that misinterpretation seems less likely. One might claim that she suffers largely because her desire to please Olive is thwarted by her yet stronger desire to please Ransom. But this makes her appear more passive than she is - even though this kind of passivity is no doubt part of her make-up, witness: "she was too free from private self-reference"

(p. 151), and even more in "she cared more for her friend's opinion of Henry Burrage than for her own" (p. 131). The complete image of Verena is more than this though. She comes to care for her own opinion of Ransom more than for her friend's. She grows, but not from Innocence to Experience. By way of illustration we have the following exchange between her and Olive - it is comic, subtle and innocent all at once: Verena has confessed to her feelings for Basil Ransom, and talks of her "shameless tolerance" of the man (almost like one of those Restoration comic heroines who perpetually disclaim all interest in men) -

> Shameless Verena admitted it to be; she assented over and over to this proposition, and explained, as eagerly each time as if it were the first, what it was that had come to pass, what it was that had brought her round (p. 329).

Again here we have James's beautiful capturing of tone and style - the precision of language reflecting just that *innocence,* just that Tarrant phraseology - for the Tarrants are always being brought on or round or started up or got going. And what was it that had brought her round?

> It had simply come over her that she liked him.

Surely one of the wittiest sentences in the novel? And the comedy of it is in no sense reductive. The fact that it is *also* comic, and not only innocent,gives it an advantage over the innocence of many of Blake's celebrated *Songs*. But one must continue the quotation:

> It had simply come over her that she liked him, that this was the true point of view, the only one from which one could consider the situation in a way that would lead to what she called a *real* solution - a permanent rest (p. 329).

There is so much more than a simple and spontaneous confession - there is her wonderful recognition of her inability to struggle against her feelings and the immense effort at frankness and honesty about them. But the full flowering of the irony (some such image is required) is still to come, in that it appears to be a recognition that Verena herself resists recognizing. In the very affirming of her love for Ransom in this way, she urges Olive to believe that what she above all wants to prove is that she can now do without him, "that a woman *could* live on persistently, clinging to a great, vivifying, redemptory idea, without the help of a man" (pp. 329-30). (How Olive must have suffered at getting her own phraseology back in this way!) This is self-deception, even comic self-deception, but at all events unconscious and therefore innocent. She cannot tread the path of full moral consciousness, committed as she is to feeling and impulse and good nature. But she is complete nevertheless, in the sense of containing contradictions, as instanced above, and in the sense of being createdly *there* for our reasons and our senses.

Surely, then, there is a James novel that ought to be much more widely appreciated, yet it is on very few lists that I have seen of required reading at British or Dutch universities. Students find James "difficult," "intellectual," "lacking in warmth, in passion," It is particularly in connexion with this last complaint that *The Bostonians* could alter his reputation as a novelist. There is no doubt a certain lack of warmth, or surface warmth at any rate, in his work, but this is an almost unavoidable consequence of his detached, ironical stance - wherein much of his greatness as an artist lies. He says some very hard things about Miss Birdseye, but who puts this novel down without a strong sense of compassion for that great muddled missionary?

Might it not be said that the artistic achievement of many a nineteenth-century novelist is to be measured by his or her ability to combine and fuse wit and passion? In that fusion is the "complete image." The Brontës, for instance, are committed to the exploring of the passions, but by and large lack wit, and so, to put it bluntly, lack perspective, to put things in new and unexpected relations with each other, to see contradictions simultaneously;[8] and this perspective is central to James, the source and life of his creative vision.

There is much in Miss Birdseye that could have made her into a tragic figure: "she had never, in her long, unrewarded, weary life, had a thought or an impulse for herself. She had been consumed by the passion of sympathy" (p. 34). Unrewarded, sacrificial, passionately sympathetic - it is a moving description - but the sentence goes on "it had crumpled her into as many creases as an old glazed, distended glove." The juxtaposition is quite extraordinary, and of course a common feature of James's art. Again, when her death is approaching - a time when we might have expected more overt sympathy from her creator, we are told that she "had given herself away so lavishly all her life that it was rather odd there was anything left of her for the supreme surrender" (p. 342). But the balance remains, the balance of sympathy for her warm-heartedness and satirical awareness of her folly; and at the same time in that reference to the "supreme surrender," dignity is restored to Miss Birdseye, much as Dickens restores dignity to Mrs Gradgrind in the farcical comedy of her death when she "took upon herself the dread solemnity of the sages and patriarchs."[9] I have called it balance, but one might do better by relating this to what Birrell says, citing I.A. Richards, "that the poet is the man who never says *less* than two things at once, and that the essence of great poetry is that it provides the reconciliation of opposites" (p. 263).

Uncomplicated warmth of feeling is perhaps something we look for in vain in James, and this is not necessarily to his discredit, but the charge of lack of passion in his works is absurd, particularly when one has Basil Ransom in mind, who, one might say, has all the dynamic of a Heathcliff, all his intensity and drive (but without his gnashing of teeth). Of the final scene in the Boston Music Hall, Birrell writes that "Basil Ransom bursts into the waiting-room" (p. 262). It is a small but interesting error of fact. That is perhaps indeed how one recalls the scene - a violent bursting in - whereas in fact he stands by passionately determined, desperately hoping, but *helpless* until Mr Filer's exasperated thumping at the door (p. 379) makes Verena open it from within. From here on one can talk metaphorically of Ransom's bursting in, perhaps, - and like a Heathcliff. Naturally I admit that the two are very different, and I do not envisage a lengthy comparison ... but it is significant that one can even *think* of Ransom in Brontë terms. And if in Brontë terms, why not in Lawrentian terms, for the example comes ready to hand in Henry in *The Fox?* Again I do not mean to try to attempt any full comparison involving two such different works, but it seems to me even more significant that two such different artists, in the essentially different ways, should both have given us this fable, this same fable of human commitment, of human desire that is ready to murder in the interests of life - for Basil Ransom is as much the murderer of Olive Chancellor as Henry is of Banford, and their reasons are the same, and their callousness. Henry's "methods" are somehow less energetic, if that is the word (in spite of the tree), but he is quite resolute, quite as subtle in his way, as Ransom, and has similar risks to take, similar problems. He is less of a Heathcliff. And he is seen from within in a way that was not James's way:

> He hoped that to-night she would stay a little while with him, after Banford had gone upstairs. He hoped he could touch her soft, creamy cheek, her strange, frightened face. He hoped he could look into her dilated, frightened dark eyes, quite near. He hoped he might even put his hand on her bosom and feel her soft breasts under her tunic. His heart beat deep and powerful as he thought of that. He wanted very much to do so.[10]

What Lawrence so admirably captures in this scene - and he develops it at (dare one say?) comic length - is the desire, the need and the helplessness of Henry at this moment. Desire, need and helplessness[11] are experienced with quite as much intensity by Ransom, though the terms are different. It might be said that in the one we have the human-animal emphasis, in the other the social-human, but the fable is the same (though the larger work has wider implications). The vision, too, of human passion and of human tenderness, I suggest, is more similar than might have been expected, at least to judge from some of the commentators on James.

If Gorley Putt, for instance, is right, then "James was inspired by the sacred terror of his own individuality."[12] The quotation is from Van Wyck Brooks, but Putt subscribes to the same opinion and affirms that this same "sacred terror of his own individuality"

> was transferred, time and time again, to his best developed characters and also to the puppets of tales about withdrawals and renunciations. Only occasionally does he dip down to his own subjective blood-springs for material directly pumped, so to say, into a created character.

If this is indeed "the germ of the matter" as Putt puts it (p. 188), then how did James ever contrive to create a Ransom - or even, for that matter, a Miss Birdseye? From what inspired source in James's make-up did *they* come? Putt's diverting suggestion that he dipped down into his own blood-springs and pumped what he found there into Olive Chancellor (!) leads one to conclude that Ransom grew out of James's masochism.

This is all wrong. Yet my own argument about Ransom and his tenderness for Verena might also be queried (though it is demonstrably there); and the final sentence of the novel has made more than one reader doubt Ransom's merits as a future husband: Verena is in tears, and it

> is to be feared that with the union, so far from brilliant, into which she was about to enter, these were not the last which she was destined to shed.

At first sight it is a sour conclusion (and un-Lawrentian in its sourness), and, remembering Verena's pain at finding Ransom "so aggressive and unmerciful" (p. 284) during their outing in the Central Park, one might presume that marriage for her became a mere extension of this experience.But his animadversions on that occasion against the "modern world" and the Movement are referred to again later -

> the words he had spoken to her there about her genuine vocation, as distinguished from the hollow and factitious ideal with which her family and her association with Olive Chancellor had saddled her - these words, the most effective and penetrating he had uttered, had sunk into her soul and worked and fermented there. She had come at last to believe them (p. 332).

And a few lines further:

> She was to burn everything she had adored; she was to adore everything she had burned. The extraordinary part of it was that though she felt the situation to be, as I say, tremendously serious, she was not ashamed of the treachery ... she meditated.

Even in the expression of her elated "conversion" there are intimations of suffering ahead - in the "burning" and the "treachery." If at this juncture she is not ashamed, yet she is *not* a romantic heroine and is bound to have later moments of remorse in contemplating Olive's misery.

As to the tears that Ransom was to cause her, James is unambiguous about these: they are the consequence of Ransom's realistic honesty (tenderness, if you like) and her love for him:

> He allowed her, certainly, no illusion on the subject of the fate she should meet as his wife; he flung over it no rosiness of promised ease; he let her know that she should be poor, withdrawn from view, a partner of his struggles, of his severe, hard, unique stoicism. When he spoke of such things as these, and bent his eyes on her, she could not keep the tears from her own; she felt that to throw herself into his life (bare

> and arid as for the time it was), was the condition of happiness for her, and yet that the obstacles were terrible, cruel. It must not be thought that the revolution which was taking place in her was unaccompanied with suffering (p. 333).

To say that a condition of happiness on this earth is the acceptance of some tears and suffering is not to say anything very sour.

University of Groningen D.R.M. Wilkinson

NOTES

1 "The Greatness of *The Bostonians,*" DQR, vol. 7, 1977/ 4, 242-264. Further quotations from Birrell are from this article.
2 This is a rough paraphrase of Blake's "To Generalize is to be an Idiot" from his annotations to Reynold's *Discourses.*
3 Elizabeth Schultz, "*The Bostonians:* the Contagion of Romantic Illusion," in *Genre,* 4 (March 1971), 45-59.
4 Theodore C. Miller, "The Muddled Politics of Henry James's *The Bostonians,*" in the *Georgia Review,* 26 (Fall, 1972), 336-46.
5 Kenneth Graham, *Henry James: the Drama of Fulfilment* (Oxford: Clarendon Press, 1975), p. 79. In a recent discussion he made it clear to me that his views are far from "black and white" now.
6 Henry James, *The Bostonians* (Penguin Books, 1966), p. 232. All further page references are to this edition.
7 It could also be argued that Ransom is rather innocent.
8 More and more these days people are seeing 'social perspective' in the Brontës' work. What I am concerned with here is the effect of their lack of wit.
9 *Hard Times,* the conclusion to Bk. II, ch. IX.
10 D.H. Lawrence, "The Fox," in *The Short Novels,* Vol. I. (London: Heinemann, 1956), p. 45. Further page references are to this edition.
11 In both their poverty is an added hindrance to the achievement of their desires.
12 S. Gorley Putt, *A Reader's Guide to Henry James* (London: Thames and Hudson, 1966), p. 188.

FROM PLEACHED GARDEN TO JUNGLE AND WASTE LAND: HENRY JAMES'S BEAST

James's nouvelle, "The beast in the Jungle" (1903; 1909 N.Y. Edition), has been called a "harrowing" story. It has been read as the story of an egotist who unwittingly misses his chance for happiness and loses - to death - the woman who loves him. The nouvelle is surely this, but more. It echoes for many readers throughout their lives as an uncomfortable moral and practical reminder of how one's self can circle the clearing in the jungle, waiting for the beast to jump. John Marcher devotes his life to his faith that one day the beast will leap. What the leap will mean, how he is to act at the great moment, he does not know, nor does his companion-in-waiting, May Bartram, who is his only confidant and his partner, not his wife, in the long vigil. Marcher (who scarcely seems to move) is so obsessed with the one special treasure he has, the waiting for the springing beast, that his life sounds like Prufrock observing Ash Wednesday, but the tiger is pre-Christian.

We have met Marcher and Prufrock, say, in Byron's *Don Juan* and in Kierkegaard and in Camus. He is Don Quixote without a windmill, horse or lance. He waits for a great and meaningful event and only rarely dares to create it or face it himself. What is worse, he refuses to see in the daily routine of ordinary life the possible resolution for the waiting. Our heroes of emptiness don't often use a gun. They, like Marcher, fret and nag their lives away in minute self-attentiveness and expectation, demanding others join them in their preoccupation and thereby draining them too of life and joy. The victims may be masochists but their intentions, like those famous ones of parents, are good. They think "love" *is* enough. The Marchers, Don Juans, the Prufrocks, the Werthers do not. At least not love which involves attention to work, meals, children, illness, small pleasures. They fear the women who would tame the beast: make it domestic, unromantic, controlled, just as the jungle landscape has become an urbanized waste land. Since they cannot live without these women, they turn them into the enemy, the danger. This impossibly complex relationship and need is perhaps what makes James's point of view so uncertain in "The Beast in the Jungle" and the critics so divided in their appraisals.

Marcher, then, is the paralyzed protagonist caught in a no-man's land he himself has invented, a clearing in a jungle never charted. Is there a study waiting to be written on the special ability of American authors to create such a waste land as seen by asexual or obsessive city dwellers? Henry James here domesticates it in London. Eliot's is urban and Fitzgerald's *The Great Gatsby* has a train track run through the ashes from suburb to city. When we recall the dialogue between Jake Barnes, war casualty steer of *The Sun Also Rises,* and his friend Bill, a mixture of Babbitt's embarrassing man-talk and twenties' humour, the literary cross-references begin to sound like a graduate school examination. Bill says of Jake's "accident:" "That's the sort of thing that can't be spoken of. That's what you ought to work up into a mystery, like Henry's bicycle." Jake protests: "He was riding horseback." Before Henry James and his mysterious injury are dropped from the conversation Bill adds, "I think he's a good writer, too." Later in the novel Jake, drunk and unable to sleep, reads one of the stories in Turgenieff's *A Sportsman's Sketches*. "I had read it before, but it seemed quite new." While Jake is trying to establish some meaning and code for his life as his eyes follow the text, the jungle, bull and Christian fiesta are being prepared outside his hotel room. When I suggested that "The Beast in the Jungle" becomes for many readers a part of their private vocabulary I mean what Jake, the admirer of James who in turn was so fond of Turgenieff as a man and as a writer, says:

> I read the Turgenieff. I knew that now, reading it in the oversensitized state of my mind after too much brandy, I would remember it somewhere, and afterward it would seem as though it had really happened to me. *I would always have it. That was another good thing you paid for and had* (italics added).

Perhaps the American waste landers are just regional examples of a western literary phenomenon. We may rail against this figure in the carpet - another Jamesian addition to our vocabulary - by evoking a Dickens, a Bellow. But it is too pervasive and too painful a landscape: there is no important writer, including these, in the history of the novel who does not describe it and invent a character to live in his fiction.

In "The Beast in the Jungle" James convinces us to accept a sad paradigm for a truth about life: in fear of being nobody, we cling to one eccentricity, one hope to give ourselves some kind of distinction and special shape. He suggests we then find a partner who is willing to go into hiding, watch in the blind for the great happening which will surely occur. It never does. But wearing our safari clothes under our normal attire we follow the chase. All around us are fertile areas for work, for self-expression and growth, but some of us have the hunter's urge. We stalk the beast of ourselves, glorying in our misplaced devotion and bravery.

How does Mary Bartram become nurse and platonic lover to Marcher of the at first harmless fantasy? Why does she stay with him when she realizes the fantasy is turning cancerous, eating up herself and him? All the critics have pointed out she must be in love with him. She is. But near the end of her life, in April "the cruellest month" but also when the tiger springs and "us he devours," May has been changed, transformed (as Marcher the untouched has not). She receives her old friend in front of her last fire on a sad spring day. Her aspect matches this setting where she tries to show his sterile love its own sterility.

> Almost as white as wax, with the marks and signs in her face as numerous and as fine as if they had been etched by a needle, with soft white draperies relieved by a faded green scarf on the delicate tone of which the years had further refined, she was the picture of a serene and exquisite but impenetrable sphinx, whose head, or indeed all whose person, might have been powdered with silver. She was a sphinx, yet with her white petals and green fronds she might have been a lily too - only an artificial lily, wonderfully imitated and constantly kept, without dust or stain, though not exempt from a slight droop and a complexity of faint creases, under some clear glass bell.

Here is Marcher's companion, scarred and fragile, in her winding clothes. At the end of the story he even thinks she might have recovered if he had acted and cured her with love. But *she* is the beast who tried to spring and in years of waiting for her cue to leap found the hunter staring inward, rather than at the arena. May is a sphinx, an artificial lily, a woman become slowly a monster, waiting to be born, not to give birth. Marcher's ignorance of what he should have noticed - the vitality and leaping grace of May, her intelligence and loyalty, all seen by him as something he has somehow earned, deserved - leads to May's death, the beast diminished to fit a polite grave.

James uses metaphors linking Marcher with crippledness and May with animality, albeit restrained. Masks are attached to both of them.[1] How can an emotionally crippled man recognize the healthy animal in a woman? Or does May Bartram sicken, grow maimed under Marcher's restrictedness? That Marcher is fuzzy-memoried we learn at once. He had told May his "secret" when she was twenty and he twenty-five. She recalls every detail of that confession, he does not. He even forgets he has told her. If there is an incredible as well as weak touch in the nouvelle it comes here. How and why does Marcher forget for ten years having bared his life's purpose, held since childhood, to a comparative stranger? Does James make him a temporary amnesiac just to permit May to grow old and solitary enough to act as the one who enables Marcher to fuse to some extent with another human being? Or is Marcher so self-involved that he suffers from the half-man's usual symptoms: selective memory, selective use of the senses? The reader is left to choose his own answer. Perhaps the most sensible is that James is as fond of plot twists and suspension of logic as the next writer.

So the renewal of May and Marcher's acquaintance leads him to describe once more his belief and to hear for the first time May query it. She will continue to do so subtly and then more openly in the years that follow. But now at thirty and a companion-tour guide (her future career with Marcher is foretold) for wealthy relatives, she inquires:

> "It's to be something you're merely to suffer?"
> "Well, say to wait for - to have to meet, to face,to see suddenly break out of my life; possibly destroying all further consciousness, possibly annihilating me; possibly, on the other hand, only altering everything, striking at the root of all my world and leaving me to the consequences, however they shape themselves."

This is Marcher's expansion of his preceding claim: "It hasn't yet come. Only, you know, it isn't anything I'm to *do*, to achieve in the world, to be distinguished or admired for. I'm not such an ass as *that*. It would be much better, no doubt, if I were." How fine he feels he is in his rejection of ordinary goals, as he hides behind an ordinary mask of routine mediocrity! May asks if the danger he faces is falling in love. He of course denies it, asserting he has been in love and not met the beast. May is sure that he has not really known love.

John Marcher's self-deprecation, humility, adolescent faith are proof that he *is* an ass. May, now with a small inheritance, sets up house in London and the pattern of their lives becomes an airless relationship of theatre, opera, small suppers, small gifts. Nevertheless, May the woman-as-therapist, offers Marcher more air than he has ever breathed. He learns something of sharing even though he prides himself on the rational balance of the friendship while the reader is aware it is really May who creates it. His stubbornness remains: "a man of feeling didn't cause himself to be accompanied by a lady on a tiger hunt."

Marcher thinks he is not really hurting his woman. Marcher "handsomely" decides not to talk about the beast all the time. Yet, "such a feature in one's outlook was really like a hump on one's back ... One discussed of course *like* a hunchback, for there was always, if nothing else, the hunchback face."

Not only has Marcher a "hunchback face" but James says he sees himself as "the most harmless of maniacs" and as having "a screw loose." The point of view all through the nouvelle seems to be Marcher's, with only several telling authorial asides. May continues to play therapist, her help seen through Marcher's eyes.

> He knew how he felt, but, besides knowing that, she knew how he *looked* as well; he knew each of the things of importance he was insidiously kept from doing, but she could add up the amount they made, understand how much, with a lighter weight on his spirit, he might have done, and thereby establish how, clever as he was, he fell short.

The reader groans at the "insidiously;" in fact, the whole passage has an air of genteel paranoia. Here is where the Jamesian "point of view" is most effective, in enabling his character to invoke both his own and our separate judgment without extra commentary. Marcher even prides himself on his "long act of dissimulation" in fooling society about the true tie between May and himself. We know they are the crippled spectators, the mutual killers. He is pleased to believe that "What it had come to was that he wore a mask painted with the social simper, out of the eyeholes of which there looked eyes of an expression not in the least matching the other features." He gloats - surely that is the tone of the proud male who feels he gives a meaning in life to a humble female - when he notes "It was only May Bartram who had, and ... achieved, by an art indescribable, the feat of at once - or perhaps it was only alternately - meeting the eyes from in front and mingling her own vision, as from over his shoulder, with their peep through the apertures." Generous point of view! May can share, May too can wear the beast's mask and search for the beast! What is most generous, of course, is the chance for the reader to perceive all these points through the mask too.

What May, the woman, thinks about their time in the bush is given to us only through Marcher's thoughts. James implies the cost of the intense ritual to May:

> She did watch with him, and she let this association give shape and colour to her own existence. Beneath *her* forms as well detachment had learned to sit, and behaviour had become for her, in the social sense, a false account of herself. There was but one account of her that would have been true all the while and that she could give straight to nobody, least of all to John Marcher.

Further, we read with a recognition of our original sense of Marcher's narrow self-involvement: "Her whole attitude was a virtual statement, but the perception of that only seemed called to take its place for him as one of the many things necessarily crowded out of his consciousness."

May cooperates (in Marcher's eyes she even is well-compensated and saved from "unintelligent society") with Marcher's treatment of her as a favoured servant at his altar. She even strengthens our sense of the religious quality of his fanaticism when she comments, "I'm your dull woman, a part of the daily bread for which you pray at church." James has developed a warm, perceptive young woman into a masked, wrinkle-etched middle-aged staple of her man's diet. She has become the beast in two ways. May is less than human in her self-inhibiting, careful faithfulness. May is also a beast who has caged and killed her emotions and can leap only as a ghost when it is impossible for Marcher to catch her.

"The Beast in the Jungle" is a ghost story and a more frightening one than "The Turn of the Screw." As in the latter, there is a secret, there is hidden sexuality, there is death with no clear medical diagnosis. The dead May haunts the living Marcher as she never could or did living. When alive she attempts several times to protect Marcher from the fate she correctly foresees: a loss of faith in his special case and a suffering that comes too late to be assuaged. He will be left in the empty space of himself as he always had been, except when she, mother, sister, wife, kept him company, stilled his fears, exaggerated his stature as a man. After her death there is no consolation, private or social, for a man who has avoided life. In the middle years of their friendship, when Marcher fears he has lost even fear (his only true emotion) and that the beast has slunk away, May pumps up his emptiness by reassuring him, when he suspects she knows much more about the beast than he, with the terrible ominous words, "You'll never find out." In a true ghost story we "never find out." Perhaps that is why this nouvelle asks for some of us, in its indefinite horror, many of our own hidden questions. And that is why "The Jolly Corner" is by contrast to the two already mentioned such a "healthy" story in that the ghost element is "found."

Marcher thinks of May, "She might have finer nerves ... [women's] nerves, their sensibility, their imagination, were conductors and revealers ...." Marcher does not have finer nerves. James in an authorial comment indicates that Marcher begins to worry whether the crisis of her illness is that catastrophe which he has awaited. As he worries about his "personal privation" he finds again his "agreeable" equanimity. The words James uses are among the most brutal in his prose - how well observed is this simple description, not of egotism, but of male arrogance at its worst. Marcher thinks, in "one of those partial recoveries" at this moment when a normal person might sorrow, that "it showed him that what was still first in his mind was the loss she herself might suffer." What is that loss? Marcher can worry only about his dear subservient companion thus: "What if she should have to die before knowing, before seeing-?" With another turn of the knife James reveals the open flesh and blood anatomy of human relationships as he exposes Marcher. "These reflections, as I say, quickened his generosity ...." How sorry he is that May must die without having experienced the great event, the meeting with the beast. He is, James says, surprised at this disturbance of his and her life pattern; in fact it gave him "almost the only positive surprise ... his career, if career it could be called, had yet offered him." James is clear here in his loathing, certainly not too strong a word, for his "hero." May now surprises Marcher in many ways. His vanity is struck by her looking old. If May is old, so is Marcher. If May dies, then all is too late, all is failure. If he is no longer young then he is, in James's words, stale and weak, "the secret of the Gods had grown faint, had perhaps even evaporated ...." His vanity, his arrogance, his self-commitment remain intact as he faces May's act of "betrayal," her illness and death. "He had but one desire left - that he shouldn't have been 'sold'."

The nouvelle could end here, with perhaps even section IV added, where May, dying, tells Marcher that what she has never said might be "more monstrous than all the monstrosities we have named." Does she lie to him when she rises from her chair with difficulty, her charm cold but almost that of youth again, and assures him he will never "consciously suffer?" She comforts and teaches him, woman in the traditional sense, to the end.

There is more to come. It may sound obvious, mechanical, but James holds us with the unanswered question: Who is the Beast? The Sphinx? Marcher decides, as May lies dying, that the Beast is the stamp of the common doom: solitude, loss, death. And he feels that is a dreadful enough discovery. May, in their final meeting, will not, again the comforting woman, leave him with this "common doom." She puts her hand on his (the only time in the nouvelle we actually see them touch) and she speaks as to a "sick child" and as a "sybil" (two other roles women play for their men) and maintains "it" has already happened, he has no more to fear. She forbids him to suffer, since the expected event of his life is long past. Throughout these pages the reader is tempted to scrawl "unclear" in the margins of the text but it is James who matches our impatience against Marcher's. The little-boy wonder is still part of Marcher in his later years so that he can, unbelievably, ask May if his secret, which only she has "penetrated," has been "too much." "Is it of that then you're dying?" Not even May's death is her own. It is part of Marcher's obsession, not her own agony at all. He even tears from her - or to be fair she tears from herself - the cry, "I would live for you still - if I could .... But I can't!"

Marcher is left to face May's death and funeral doubly bereaved. She is gone and he has no official status as her mourner. We see the real scar the Beast has given him, the worst scar of all. It is that he is unmarked, he is the invisible lover, the invisible lover, the ignored and the untouched. What greater horror can there be? The man who protects himself from being marked by life, through an amorphous and unspecified fear of vanity or self-delusion is the man whose own untouched face is his most dreadful mask. The Beast has sprung yet its claws have not deigned to gash the victim.

Here is Marcher's fate, the fate of the man too in love with himself and his own goals, to love another:

> What it presently came to in truth was that poor Marcher waded through his beaten grass, where no life stirred, where no breath sounded, where no evil eye seemed to gleam from a possible lair, very much as if vaguely looking for the Beast, and still more as if acutely missing it. He walked about in an existence that had grown strangely more spacious, and, stopping fitfully in places where the undergrowth of life struck him as closer, asked himself yearningly, wondered secretely and sorely, if it would have lurked here or there. It would have at all events *sprung;* what was at least complete was his belief in the truth of the assurance given him. The change from his old sense to his new was absolute and final: what was to happen *had* so absolutely and finally happened that he was as little able to know a fear for his future as to know a hope; so absent in short was any question of anything still to come. He was to live entirely

> with the other question, that of his unidentified past, that of his having to see his fortune impenetrably muffled and masked.

Marcher remains as self-romanticizing and self-focussed as ever. "The torment of this vision became then his occupation ...." James knows so well these self-involved preoccupations: What did *I* once have, what do *I* have now, what shall *I* do? What is most satisfying to *me?*

A pilgrimage to the "grim suburban metropolis" with its "wilderness of tombs" precedes Marcher's year's journey to the East in an attempt to recover his consciousness of the Beast. He waits for the stones of May's grave to pity him (where is his pity for her?) and to reveal her secret knowledge of the Beast. But "in vain; they kept what they concealed; and if the face of the tomb did become a face to him it was because her two names were like a pair of eyes that didn't know him. He gave them a last long look, but no palest light broke." May is both the Beast and its ghost taunting Marcher with the mask he once was so proud to wear, to have her wear.

James, like the eyes of the gravestone, does not let us go. Though Marcher is still tormented, he is not made to repeat his tale to any unlucky passerby. Instead, it is James who nags and nags, in his writer's perfectionist drive, at the unhappy Marcher. He is now truly a romantic character in his own eyes, an aged man inventing his own gorgeous past, bored by the exotic worlds he finds "vulgar and vain," elevating May's grave to "his own witness of a past glory." What past glory? What great adventures? Marcher invents a crowded life but in reality only "this garden of death gave him the few square feet of earth on which he could still most live." So: a man can live a life propelled by a secret and find himself with only another person's grave to give him any meaning, any sense of dignity. But James is not content with this punishment, this fate he creates for his character. "Thus in short he settled to live - feeding all on the sense that he once *had* lived, and dependent on it not alone for a support but for an identity." James adds that Marcher is still deluded, still believes a relevation will come, and James's words are as cutting as the pain Marcher feels in the autumn that brings the novel full circle to its seasonal beginning at Weatherend. What pitying contempt: "He was to live to believe this [the coming of the light, the truth], I say, though he was not to live, I may not less definitely mention, to do much else."

The light does break. Marcher sees it in the fact of another mourner in the cemetery. The smooth habit of Marcher's sorrowing visits now melts in the glare of that ravaged face. Thorns have pierced the other and left Marcher untouched. "What had the man *had,* to make him by the loss of it so bleed and yet live?" Only a man who had never himself fallen upon the cutting edge of experience could ask such a Shelleyean question.

In the final paragraph James's verbs flame up to illuminate "John Marcher's arid end." He stands gazing at "the sounded void of his life." The Beast, he now believes, was as we knew a romantically exaggerated animal. The fate he had been marked for he had met with a vengeance - he had emptied the cup to the lees; he had been the man of his time, *the* man to whom nothing on earth was to have happened. Marcher is left in 'pale horror'. Waiting has been the horror; marriage with May a possible escape from the horror. The horror of waking and of knowledge are the final marks of the Beast. May "had prayed he mightn't know" that he is nothing, a vacuum, a suicide who walked through life unaware of his own death.

Does our hero change as the sorrow-blazed face of the stranger leads him to knowledge? No. No more than the finely wrinkled face of May changed his life, led him to notice others, to be aware of himself in human relationships and in work. His last action finds him still a coward, still fearful of deeper understanding and painful self-analysis. Not even his imagined sentimental solution, marriage with May (the accepted way of reading this nouvelle), makes all end happily with a character redeemed by self-knowledge. Marcher clings to his old self to the end, turning away from horror and sorrow and the "common doom."

> He saw the Jungle of his life and saw the lurking Beast; then, while he looked, perceived it, as by a stir of the air, rise, huge and hideous, for the leap that was to settle him. His eyes darkened - it was close; and, instinctively turning, in his hallucination, to avoid it, he flung himself face down, on the tomb.

Poor May, the woman whose breast had to become hard stone to receive her frightened friend. Marcher's Beast was familiar to May. Why a woman hides such knowledge is James's implicit query answered only partially by the much too easy explanation: she loved him. She did, perhaps. And perhaps she was, as we have indicated, infected through the long years with Marcher's fear of suffering, the Beast in us. That fear paralyzes us from living, from will, from passion, from action. We will never meet and conquer the Beast if our faces turn to avoid it. Like May and Marcher we will sicken delicately and emptily, the Beast gnawing in silence within. Perhaps if we recognize the Beast and make it part of our lives we can exist in the Jungle, the wild and the tamed in balance.

Recall May's words to Marcher, "I'm your dull woman, part of the daily bread ...." Match these against Marcher's sense of his fate after May's death: "his having to see his fortune impenetrably muffled and masked." In a poem James surely knew similar words point up the nouvelle's dilemma. Like "The Beast in the Jungle" this poem seems to be to resonate through American Literature and abroad. F.O.Matthiessen pays it special attention in *American Renaissance,* for which we must be grateful since few readers would go unguided today to the poetry of Ralph Waldo Emerson. "Days," published in 1857 when Emerson was fifty-four celebrates the cultivated plot where Marcher might have belonged and which Henry James left, although he never forgot that pleached morality so central to his brother William's pragmatic philosophy or to his own art. William remained in Cambridge, like Emerson. Henry, as Hemingway would have it, rode horseback through Europe and England, finding his walled jungle at last, in Rye. Here is Emerson, brief enough to quote in full:

Days

Daughters of time, the hypocritic Days,
Muffled and dumb, like barefoot dervishes,
And Marching single in an endless file,
Bring diadems and fagots in their hands.
To each they offer gifts, after his will, -
Bread, kingdoms, stars, or sky that holds them all.
I, in my pleached garden, watched the pomp,
Forgot my morning wishes, hastily
Took a few herbs and apples, and the Day
Turned and departed silent. I, too late,
Under her solemn fillet saw the scorn.

That Emerson never wrote another poem as good as this does not matter. We have the poem as a précis and foreshadowing of his countryman's, the younger Henry James, special greatness, as an abstract of how James's art works. The "hypocritic" times distract us from possibilities, from the finest of moral acts. The beat of their march, the ominous procession, make some of us retreat or act foolishly or choose in haste. For James as for Emerson the jungle is an exaggerated image; the waste land is right in the back yard whenever we care to look. It is in our own clearings that the beast is recognized. May Bartram would have taken "a few herbs and apples" and have been willing to accept the scorn of the filleted day. We leave Isabel Archer running from the garden where Casper Goodwood offers her Emerson, passion, life's food. Young Maisie is wise, opts for frugality, however her heart breaks. So down the "endless file" of James's creations the Days pass in their parade with Maggie Verver at the very last smashing a golden bowl in exchange for marital honesty, for herbs and apples. Marcher of "The Beast in the Jungle" belongs with those sad James characters who play it so safe, wait so long to take their chances, ask so much of life and give so little and so humourlessly in return, that they are justly scorned. Their gardens are sterile, their loves are graves.

When we juxtapose Emerson's "Days" and James's nouvelle, we see how clearly May Bartram *is* the "Sphinx," as James called her. She will not answer Marcher; it is he who must answer her riddle. Marcher should have seen that the reply to the Sphinx's riddle is a description of a man. Then he might have entered the city and have lived and loved, and have suffered the blinding tragedy of the Waste Land, however awful. He is instead punished with "the common doom" as he remains outside, the Sphinx gazing at him stony and silent.

University of Leiden S. Betsky-Zweig

NOTE

1 James worked out some astonishing variations on these metaphors in the ghost-mask of "The Jolly Corner (and a woman who does leap to the rescue); in the eyes of Osmond watching Isabel from a window or on a coin; in the pervasive animal and bird imagery of *The Golden Bowl*.

FAULKNER'S WORLD AS THE EXTENSION OF REALITY: *AS I LAY DYING* RECONSIDERED

William Faulkner's outrageous story of the Bundren family is undoubtedly one of his most complex and enigmatic novels; complex, because beneath the surface narrative of a grotesque journey we are aware of terrifying depths of human significance; enigmatic, because we never seem to be quite certain in what sense the novel controls our responses. Is the bizarre tale of the Bundrens just macabre comedy or heart-breaking tragedy? Is it a story of heroics or does it mock heroics? Is it an epic with Addie as the dead queen and her sons as the princes carrying out their ritual duties, or does it parody epic? What makes it difficult to find the right answer to these questions is the fact of the irony that informs the novel from start to finish.[1] To appreciate the book's full riches it is therefore necessary to see how exactly the irony works, in its thematics, the characterization, as well as in its vision. Only then will we be in a position to understand that *As I Lay Dying* is at once a comedy and the reverse of comedy, a tragedy and a mockery of tragedy, an epic and the parody of epic, and that instead of detracting from the novel's power these paradoxes tend to intensify it.

With novels like *The Hamlet, The Town,* and *The Mansion, As I Lay Dying* belongs to those works in which Faulkner deals with the Southern poor whites, a group of people long associated in the popular mind with illiteracy, shiftlessness, and brutality. Faulkner did not contribute to this folklore. Although he made use of the comic possibilities of the type, he generally treats the poor whites in his works with sympathy, seeing in them a dignity and sense of values which, at first sight, seem totally incommensurate with their appalling poverty, illiteracy, and callous and cruel behaviour. A revealing example of this is provided by an episode occurring late in *As I Lay Dying*. The waggon with its stinking burden approaches Jefferson and is passing three negroes. One of them, shocked at the evil smell, expresses his sense of outrage, and Jewel fiercely curses him, but a white man who is walking in front of the negroes thinks that it is he who is being abused, and immediately takes offence. In the exchange that follows, Darl succeeds in placating the white stranger, while holding Jewel back from starting a fight. What this incident nicely illustrates is a code of honour as elaborate as any upheld by Faulkner's Southern aristocrats.[2] There is a willingness on the part of the Bundrens to apologize for an injustice done, but it must be clearly understood that they are not afraid of facing the consequences if the family honour is at stake.

This sense of family loyalty is even more striking if we remember that Darl is not exactly a believer in idealistic conduct, and that he and Jewel hate each other. The comedy inherent in the situation - the shoddy caravan, enveloped in the appalling stench, the ludicrous cause of the misunderstanding - clearly clashes with the seriousness the Bundrens attach to the issue in question, but the effect on the reader is not an easy laugh but a heightened awareness that life can be laughed at but never laughed away. And this response also applies to the journey the Bundrens undertake to carry the dead body of the mother to a distant graveyard at Jefferson. Although all the other characters in the novel outside the Bundren family circle regard the expedition as foolish and scandalous, there is, with the exception of Darl, no one in the family who opposes the long and dangerous journey. They seem united in their determination to honour the promise exacted by Addie from her husband Anse to bury her bodily remains in Jefferson, beside her father's grave, and even Darl does not shirk the family duty when he sees that his protest is of no avail. Yet, here again, the issues are not as simple as they look. Anse's reply to the question why he is determined to take Addie's body to Jefferson is invariably: "It's Addie I give the promise to .... Her mind is set on it";[3] but there are, as we learn early in the novel, other motivations than mere obedience to the family honour. When Addie dies, Darl imagines Anse saying, "God's will be done .... Now I can get them teeth" (p. 47), an observation which proves only too true, as the end of the novel shows. Dewey Dell, the daughter, has also more than one reason: she knows that she is pregnant, and is desperate to get into town, so that she can buy drugs to effect an abortion. And even to the solid Cash the town presents temptations beyond the call of duty. Yet it is Cash, the meticulous craftsman in the family, and Jewel, the fierce, unthinking man of action, whose motivations in undertaking the expedition are most pure, and the fact that they were Addie's favourite sons may be significant in explaining this. Anse himself, in motivating the trip to his neighbours, is hardly credible. Considering his mean selfishness, his blatant hypocrisy, his inertia, one must distrust any form of piety on his part. Beside the set of teeth he longs to have, there is still another secret motive that drives him to town: he wants a new wife to replace Addie. Moreover, Anse can easily impress his neighbours with his concern for Addie, since he knows that he can depend on others to honour his promise. He knows that he can rely on his sons Cash and Jewel, and on other people as well. As he tells Cash: "I reckon there are Christians here" (p. 222). Christians, who will even lend him the spades to dig Addie's grave, so why should he bother to bring them himself?

Anse is the consummate manipulator of men, who knows how to exploit what is good in them, although he is devoid of any himself. Yet, he gets away with it, which shows that it is impossible to dismiss even him as either a caricature or mere type. Despite the impurity of his motivation, Anse remains the driving force behind the expedition, though none of the heroism which the family have to display in bringing it to a successful end falls to him. The responsibility for this is fully shouldered by both Cash and Jewel, whose superhuman efforts to save the coffin from the raging elements fully deserve the qualification heroic. For as Cleanth Brooks has remarked, "heroism is heroism even though it sometimes appears to be merely the hither side of folly" (p. 166) . The incredible feats performed by Cash and Jewel in getting the waggon and coffin safely across the flooded river leave no doubt that what we are made to witness here pertains to the epic mode. The description of the crossing itself is brilliantly done. Faulkner's technique enables us to watch it from different points of view, and the composite picture that is thus built up in the reader's mind acquires a larger-than-life vividness and intensity, without its losing touch with reality though. We not only see the events through the eyes of such a level-headed outsider as Tull, whose objective account reveals that the threat the flooded river poses is real enough; we also see them through the keyed-up, though observant imagination of Darl, whose perceptions are always coloured by a touch of the poetic, while the wild agony that the near-loss of the coffin engenders is conveyed through the child Vardaman, who frantically watches it slipping off into the water. No one, then, possesses the whole truth of what really happens, but the sum of their subjective truths lends the reality of the event a scope and depth which it cannot possibly have for those who are directly involved. In this sense art adds a dimension to reality of which the individual in confrontation with his daily existence remains unaware. Cash as well as Jewel are totally ignorant of the fact that what they achieve during the crossing is heroic; to them it is to all appearances the reverse of heroic. The same applies to the comedy that attaches to Cash, sitting on the shore with a broken leg, surrounded by his tools, dived up by a tireless Jewel, who will not think of giving up. It is again a comedy that must escape both Cash and Jewel; to them the whole sequence of catastrophic events is the reverse of comedy. But the heroics and the comedy are there, depending upon the perspective under which the events are viewed, a perspective supplied by art, because Faulkner's technique of multiple presentation of view points prevents it from cancelling those other perspectives which contradict the heroic and the comic. What this achieves for the novel is a density of texture which neither the overtly comic nor the tragic-heroic mode could have given to the writing.

Although both Cash and Jewel seem to emerge from these exploits as mere stock-characters - Cash exemplifying unreflective endurance, Jewel, brainless heroism - the picture is again much more subtle. Jewel is certainly one of the least reflective among the members of the family: of the fifty-nine sections in the novel he is given only one section in which he directly addresses the reader.

Yet we get a fairly complete view of Jewel's character; mainly through Darl's eyes, it is true - and Darl is not always to be trusted - but observations of other characters help to rectify this. Faulkner's technique of multiple presentation works admirably here, as, for that matter, it does in his characterization of the other members of the Bundren family. Jewel, then, ignorant, intolerant, and highly strung, is more than a mere automaton. His most precious possession is his horse, for which he has worked so hard that it has nearly ruined his health, and when he allows it to be sold so that the journey to Jefferson can be continued, he makes a sacrifice which reveals unexpected depths of character. But Jewel can only express his feelings through violent and brutal action. His is an unreflective, aggressive masculinity, the stuff epic heroes were made of, and he is destined to perform acts which can either be qualified as heroic (the river-crossing, the barn-burning episode), or as brutal (at the end of the novel when he jumps Darl in order to turn him over to the officers). What makes him recognizable against his Southern background of poor-white stock is the fierce hatred behind all his actions, expressing itself in the ugly violence, engendered not only by the grief about his mother's death, but also in something in his love for Addie which he could never allow himself to become conscious of: the element of incestuous desire.

Like Jewel, Cash is a man of action, and like Jewel he is one of Addie's favourite sons. But there the similarities end. Although Cash, the patient, conscientious craftsman, whose only concern seems to be his tools, begins as a comic figure, and although comedy is always just round the corner when the action involves him, his character shows him for what he certainly is: a quiet, simple and limited man, unimaginative but practical, the solid workman, but as Faulkner makes us look at him from a number of angles, it becomes necessary to modify this verdict considerably. He is unselfish in a quiet, unobtrusive way; the values he believes in may be simple and direct, but he shows dignity and integrity. When a member of the family needs help, he believes that one helps him as a matter of course, without making any fuss about it; one does not set fire to a man's barn, even if one seems to have a valid motive, and one does not help arrest a member of one's own family, as Jewel and Dewey Dell do, even if one agrees that Darl ought to be locked up in an asylum, for his own good, as Cash thinks. His most impressive qualities, however, are his great powers to endure and to suffer without complaining. With his broken leg he rides for six days on a waggon without springs, and does not give so much as a whimper. And when Dr Peabody expresses his sarcastic indignation about his family's stupidity - they set his leg in a cast by pouring sand and cement around it - he defends this appalling treatment by meekly pointing out that "They just aimed to ease hit some ..." (p. 227).

Dr Peabody's attitude towards Cash is a mixture of amazement, irritation, pity and secret admiration, and one can well understand and share his exasperation, which extends to the other members of the family as well, in particular to the daughter Dewey Dell, the only female character on the seat of the evil-smelling waggon. She, too, looks at first glance like a simple and rather stupid country girl, an easy victim, but like Cash she shows more depth, subtlety, and dignity of character than the circumstances we find her in at the beginning of the novel would lead us to expect. She seems entirely locked up in herself, but there are reasons. Her problem, about which she can only talk with a woman, becomes an obsession after Addie's death, leaving her no time to indulge her grief for her mother. "I wish to have time to let her die," she says, and the Shakespearean echo fittingly intensifies the agony expressed through these words. It's not that she easily accepts the idea of an abortion. As she desperately cries: "I believe in God, God. God, I believe in God" (p. 109), but her pregnancy comes too soon, "it is because in the wild and outraged earth too soon too soon too soon" (p. 107). She could have turned to Dr Peabody, but her fear and shyness prevent her from doing so. She knows that Darl has discovered that she must be pregnant, but she dislikes him, because she is afraid of his cold, observant intelligence. She is desperately alone and helpless in her confused condition and feels like "a wet seed wild in the hot blind earth" (p. 58). She has to find her own solution for what she calls "the female trouble," and her excursions to the two druggists provide high comedy, without, however, cancelling the poignant pathos of her pitiable situation.

What Dewey Dell exemplifies is the extreme isolation in which all the members of the Bundren family have to come to terms with the death of the mother, the centre which held them together and round which their existence revolved. Their ignorance and inarticulateness prevent them from sharing an experience as profound and uprooting as the death of the mother, and each responds in his own confused and isolating way. Cash, by laying his heart and soul in the making of the coffin, sawing and hammering away under the window of the dying Addie, the rain soaking his clothes; Jewel, through violent,undirected action; Dewey Dell, by frantically concentrating on finding her abortion drugs; Vardaman, the child, by simply refusing to accept his mother's death. He blames Dr Peabody for it, seeing a causal connection between him and her death, as the physician's arrival coincided with the moment she died. He bores holes in the coffin to allow Addie to breathe, and finally identifies her with the fish he had killed at about the same moment that she had passed away, an analogy which in his pre-logical, magical way of thinking begins to constitute a case of transubstantiation, guaranteeing his mother's survival: "And to-morrow it will be cooked and et and she will be him and pa and Cash and Dewey Dell and there won't be anything in the box and so she can breathe" (p. 60). Vardaman's frantic denial of his mother's death, his attempt to liberate her from the coffin, is of course strange, but the boy himself is not an imbecile. It's his way of trying to cope with the terrible shock until he can regain a hold on reality and move towards sanity again. And from his monologues it clearly appears that this process accelerates his attempts at discovering his identity, which, formless as it still is, needs definite shape if he is to make any sense of the disorder he suddenly faces. That in this search for identity he is strictly limited to the narrow circle of a family that has lost its centre of gravity, only adds to the state of utter confusion in which he gropingly tries to find his way, but the family is all he has, and when at the end of the novel even this falls apart, his emotional stress finds poignant expression in the compulsive reiteration of his mad brother's name when he cries out: "Darl is my brother. Darl. Darl" (p. 240).

If Addie's death forces the child Vardaman to become trapped in a search for identity that comes too early to be anything but painful and unhingeing, the effect on Darl is even more disastrous: his identity dissolves in madness. The importance of Darl's presence in the novel is unmistakable. In nineteen sections, the greatest number alotted to one single character, we hear his voice, and he is undoubtedly the principal narrator of the book. With Darl's gifts of observation and expression - he is by far the most articulate of the Bundrens - this is not surprising. He represents most strongly Faulkner's own detachment and insight. It is through him that we are most completely informed of the development of the narrative as well as of the hidden motivations that guide the Bundrens' behaviour. Darl sees through his father's hypocrisy, he feels intuitively that Dewey Dell is pregnant, and that Jewel is not Addie's legitimate son. This is not to say that only Darl's view is true - Faulkner's multiple presentation of view points guards us from making this mistake - but the truth he possesses lends a singular depth to the novel. The scene of Addie's death, so convincing in its fine, realistic detail, and the fantastic scene in which Cash works in the rain on the coffin, are imagined by Darl while he is away from home, but there is no reason to suspect that they are not true. They have the truth of the artist's imaginative empathy. But because he is so uncannily perceptive, he sees and knows *too* much, and of all the members of the Bundren family Darl's sense of isolation and alienation is greatest, plummeting to appalling depths when his mother dies. Addie has never accepted, nor loved her second son. Darl knows that he has no mother, and that therefore he cannot love her, but obviously not because he does not want to. Does he hate her? He probably does, but then as a fierce reaction to thwarted love. His setting fire to the barn can be explained by his desire to avenge himself on Addie, but also as an act of piety to end the undignified dragging about of the stinking corpse. That Darl sought his mother's love becomes clear from his relations with Jewel, Addie's favourite son. His fascination with Jewel, however, is not only to be explained by his jealousy of Addie's love for him, but also by his jealousy of Jewel's personality, the man of action, whose firm sense of identity he envies. Jewel knows who he is, Darl says; he, Darl not only doubts his identity, he doubts his very existence: "I dont know what I am, I dont know if I am or not" (p. 73).

Darl is unable to find in life a stable relationship with the world, probably because he has never found it in his relations with his mother. It explains his feeling of not belonging. As Cash perceptively observes: "This world is not his world; this life his life" (p. 248). Darl's tragedy is that he is intensely aware of his predicament, as is shown in his obsession with nothingness and dissolution. After the death of the only person who in some way or other still linked him to the world, even if only in a negative, destructive sense, this obsession grows to such a pitch that the difference between objective and subjective reality ceases to exist for him and he goes mad, laughing with the laughter of the mad, but still in possession of that peculiar lucidity sometimes attached to madness. In the last section that is attributed to Darl, written, significantly enough, not in the first person but in the third to indicate the complete disintegration of Darl's personality, three answers to the question why he laughs are given. They all consist of a crescendo of "yesses," and the bitter irony in these exultant affirmations movingly conveys the tragedy of his mental breakdown, for his laughter becomes the tears which he cannot shed, and who wants to affirm that the only reality women have is in their backs, and that the terrible truth is that Darl is *not* "our brother"?

Not only does Darl have no mother, he does not have a father either. Anse Bundren, as Cleanth Brooks has said, is one of Faulkner's most accomplished villians. He is also one of the most comic, but the outrageous humor with which Faulkner has drawn his character should not make us forget how dangerous he really is. Behind his unbelievable laziness, his crass egoism and despicable stinginess, there hides a predatoriness, which is made even more lethal by his consummate hypocrisy and his relentless knowledge of how far he can go in taking advantage of other people's goodness. Jewel's love of his horse, for which he has worked so back-breakingly hard that it has made his mother cry; Dewey Dell's desperate pleading to let her keep the ten dollars for the abortion drugs, mean nothing to him if they interfere with his own plans. During Addie's illness his stinginess makes him wait till the last moment before calling the doctor, and Cash's sufferings after he has broken his leg leave him completely indifferent. Yet, though he seems contemptible in practically everything he says and does, he is a man who cannot be ignored. He represents, as Cleanth Brooks has again astutely observed, "a force probably necessary to the survival of the human animal though it is terrifying when seen in such simple purity" (p. 155). And the stupendous end of the novel illustrates this better than anything else. We see him approaching the waggon, with, as Cash describes it, "that kind of daresome and hangdog look all at once like when he has been up to something he knows ma ain't going to like ..." (p. 247). His new store-bought teeth are in his mouth, making him look taller and giving him a renewed vitality, and he is accompanied by a "duck-shaped" woman with "hard-looking pop eyes," whom he then introduces to his children:" 'It's Cash and Jewel and Vardaman and Dewey Dell,' [he] says, kind of hangdog and proud too, with his teeth and all, even if he wouldn't look at us. 'Meet Mrs. Bundren,' he says." Anse may have twinges of conscience but they never stop him from satisfying what he considers are his needs. And in this respect he remains very much alive, although to Addie, his first wife, he has been dead for years.

With Addie we come to the central character of the book, as can be inferred from the very title of the story, and the fact that she *is* dead for more than three quarters of the novel no doubt crowns the irony which so all-pervasively informs the writing. In her dual role of wife and mother, Addie, a strong personality, exercises absolute power over her family, even after her death. Of a passionate nature, she is torn by conflicting attitudes to life. On the one hand there is in her a strong inclination to withdraw and to preserve the separateness of her individuality, on the other an equally strong desire to reach out to the world, to reach "the burning heart of life." Before her marriage, when she was a schoolteacher, she used to hate and whip her pupils because they intruded with their noisy and impertinent presence into her separateness, but at the same time the whipping was a desperate attempt on her part to establish some kind of communion, to impress her mark on, and conversely to feel marked by the living. It is also this aching need that makes her marry Anse, a man socially and culturally her inferior - "So I took Anse," she says - believing that it would make her feel part of "the terrible blood, the red bitter blood boiling through the land" (p. 163), and trusting that she could manage to keep whole her integrity as an individual.

Life with Anse, the mean-spirited egoist, the coarse lump of inertia and ignorance, teaches her differently. It violates her separateness "over and over each day," and never as badly as when she is to bear Anse's children. Then she realizes that she is caught in a biological trap, which makes it of no importance whether she feels herself a separate individual or not. She feels "tricked by words older than Anse or love" (p. 161), and Anse might just as well be anybody else, which makes him "dead" to her although he is alive, just as her children might be any children, except Cash because he is her first, and Jewel because through him she has expressed her protest against the words that have proved empty - words like "love," which, when used by Anse, means only more offspring to work his land;or "duty," the duty to have a husband and children, but which, as Addie realizes can never be the reason of life if, as it seems, it means the starvation of one's identity.

Although Addie hardly strikes us as a woman who believes in the spiritual, there is in her an obstinate yearning for transcendence, for an existence that is not merely vegetative, an existence that not merely happens but is made to happen by the posing of a deed that will lift the individual beyond the anonymity of the passing generations. Whitfield, the minister, seems to present an opportunity to find some higher purpose in life. He becomes her lover, but when he ends the affair, Addie is thrown back on her despairing sense of emptiness within the Bundren family, with Jewel as the visible outcome of her yearning and a renewed disgust at those who merely live through words, although at this stage she also realizes that even empty words are still dangerous because they can be used to manipulate people. Whitfield's monologue, following Addie's shocking, autobiographical account, illustrates that Addie had no reason to think better of the minister than of Anse. While listening to the sermon Whitfield preaches at Addie's funeral, even the prosaic Tull feels the discrepancy between Whitfield the man of words and Whitfield the man of deeds: "His voice is bigger than him. It's like they are not the same. It's like he is one, and his voice is one, swimming on two horses side by side across the ford and coming into the house, the mud-splashed one and the one that never even got wet, triumphant and sad" (p. 83). Whitfield may feel the urge to confess his sin, but he will never really do it, only say that he will do it, and this to him, the man of words, serves as a substitute for the act itself.

Although Addie is domineering and assertive, she remains an intensely feminine woman in that she ultimately only trusts the concrete, and through her physical body tries to gain a hold on reality. But this earth-mother quality is not of the yielding and warmth-generating kind, but is only fierceness and pride, and when she feels that it drags her down in her attempts at transcedence it even becomes destructive. When Cora Tull accuses her of not being a good mother, and reproaches her for her excessive love of Jewel, saying, "There is your sin. And your punishment too. Jewel is your punishment. But where is your salvation?," Addie calmly answers, "He is my cross and he will be my salvation. He will save me from the water and from the fire. Even though I have laid down my life, he will save me" (p. 156). Cora then realizes that Addie does not refer to God but to Jewel, and shocked at what in her eyes is wilful blasphemy and sacrilege, she begs her to repeal her words and to "cast herself upon the mercy of the Lord." But Addie is adamant in her refusal. If the road to spiritual salvation is cut off for her, she will not retreat in resignation, but in defiance, exacting salvation through the very sin she is thought to have committed, a claim made good by Jewel when he saves her coffined body from the flooded river and later from the fire in the barn-burning episode. Addie may not be a good and warm and loving woman, but her unsentimental honesty with herself and her fierce vitality make her a compelling personality of great intensity, who, even after her death, continues to extend her hold on her family, until she is brought to rest next to her father's grave. And it is only through her wish to be buried beside the man who used to tell her that "the reason for living is to get ready to stay dead a long time" (p. 157), and for which she hated him, that we know that she has admitted defeat, which lends her the tragic stature that the macabre comedy of the journey so emphatically denies her.

There is no doubt that the end of *As I Lay Dying* is grim, leaving no room for any illusions. Addie's death does not change or end anything. It does not effect a catharsis in the family. It does not bring them to greater awareness, either about Addie, about the conflicts that tore her restless life apart, or about themselves. At the end of the novel we are again at the beginning, with a new Mrs Bundren, guaranteeing the survival of the species, but with Addie's unresolved conflicts transmitted to her children. Addie's sense of isolation and alienation reaches a pitch in Darl, striking him with madness; her outrage at the violation of her individuality whenever she felt life burgeoning in her, is transferred to her daughter Dewey Dell, whose desperate anxiety about feeling trapped and betrayed leaves her no time to mourn her mother's death. Even Cash and Jewel, who one does not expect to change or show greater insight or enrichment from the experience, are worse off at the end. Only Anse, the husband, has profited, and the irony here is in line with the irony of life, which does not concern itself with equity but distributes rewards or punishments regardless of our moral, or lack of moral worth. That this may give us the impression that we live in a mad world rather than in a sane one, is also in keeping with the vision that informs Faulkner's novel. Madness, like death, is never far from our consciousness in *As I Lay Dying*. The madness of the journey is matched by the madness of the elements that oppose its completion; the madness that drives the Bundrens on, their "furious attitudes," make them unwittingly perform acts of stupendous bravery and endurance but do not cancel the irresponsible folly and the wicked cruelty that accompany these deeds; the mad comedy that attaches to their vicissitudes is overpowering but does not invalidate the tragedy inherent in them. It's all there, in all its heart-breaking confusion, making us pause before the madness of human behaviour, without much greater understanding perhaps, but at least with the kind of acceptance that precludes easy attitudes; neither a sneering dismissal of the human animal, nor a sentimental optimism in the generative forces of the primitive, will reconcile us with the enigmas Faulkner's novel poses. For in the final analysis one does not feel let down by the book. It is the furious energy one feels pulsing in the writing itself that keeps us buoyed, that works as a tonic in revitalizing our sluggishness in the face of the intractable stuff life is made of.

Although the multiplicity of view points, presenting each part of the novel through the consciousness of a particular character, may create the illusion that Faulkner has disappeared as the all-powerful manipulator, it is the style which makes him visible again. Composed of a colloquial diction, freely mingled with high rhetoric, it is this style, often approaching poetry, which is largely responsible for the novel's great power.

What this language incorporates is a vision that underlies not only *As I Lay Dying* but all of Faulkner's major works, a vision which may be summarized as follows: heroism is to be found in the most unlikely places, endurance in the most unlikely people, and both may be generated by the most unlikely circumstances. While exerting himself in the most unlikely manner for the most unlikely causes, it is impossible for the individual to know the whole truth. All he can hope for is a part of the truth, distorting his perspective and bedevilling his hold on reality. The whole truth may only be known if all the separate truths are brought together, but the ability to do this demands a depth of knowledge, sensibility and wisdom which none of Faulkner's characters will ever obtain. It is here that his characters, even the plainest, attain the tragic stature usually accorded to people of greater awareness and sophistication. That they themselves may be totally unaware of this does not take away from the reality of Faulkner's world. This can be made clear by drawing an analogy suggested by the work of the philosopher Karl R. Popper. In his *Objective Knowledge* Popper distinguishes three worlds - the physical world, the subjective and psychological world, and the world of the products of the human mind (myth, fairy tales, scientific theories, poetry, art, music).[4] Each successive world presents a progressive enrichment of empirical content - an extension of reality, I would say. To explain this Popper introduces the notion of "emergence," that is, new properties and characteristics emerge as the next world extends from the preceding world, a process being complicated by the fact that the worlds continue to interact. In Faulkner's case the same distinctions can be made. We have first the physical world; Yoknapatawpha County, the South; then the subjective and psychological world: the poor whites; and next the world of the products of the mind: the novel *As I Lay Dying,* a world with new properties and characteristics, though originating from the two preceding "simpler" worlds. This is Faulkner's world, in which the South and the poor whites may not be able to recognize themselves, but the reality of which can be looked upon as the progressive enrichment of empirical content underlying their worlds. Faulkner's world as the extension of reality.

University of Groningen J. Bakker

NOTES

1 As Cleanth Brooks has written in his discussion of *As I Lay Dying:* "Faulkner has daringly mingled the grotesque and the heroic, the comic and the pathetic, pity and terror, creating a complexity of tone that has proved difficult for some readers to cope with," *(William Faulkner: The Yoknapatawpha Country,* New Haven and London: Yale University Press, 1963, p. 141. All further page references are to this edition.)

Also André Bleikasten takes this view when he writes: "That irony informs the whole design of *As I Lay Dying* is beyond dispute," *(Faulkner's As I Lay Dying,* trans. Roger Little, Bloomington/London: Indiana University Press, revised and enlarged edition, 1973, p. 8).

Bleikasten's is undoubtedly the most extensive and exhaustive study of *As I Lay Dying* to date, but although it provides many valuable insights for which one must feel indebted to him, it tends to lose focus under the sheer weight and excess of interpretation, often leading to explications like, for instance, the following: "The wagon is soon to become Charon's ferry: the river crossing, like that of the Styx or Acheron, marks the Bundrens' entry into the underworld. We are now in Death's other Kingdom" (pp. 110-11). This kind of approach seems to have become compulsory after James Joyce, but is not always meaningful.

2 I am indebted for this point to Cleanth Brooks, *William Faulkner,* p. 143.
Brooks's analysis of *As I Lay Dying* remains one of the finest and most illuminating, even if his emphasis on the nature of the heroic as the principal theme of the story does not entirely convince.

3 William Faulkner, *As I Lay Dying* (London: Chatto & Windus, 1962), p. 102. All further page references are to this edition.

4 Karl R. Popper, *Objective Knowledge: An Evolutionary Approach* (London: Oxford University Press, 1972). See in particular Chapter 4, pp. 153-91.

THE NIGHT CAFÉ

Vincent van Gogh

Yale University Art Gallery

Bequest of Stephen Carlton Clark, B.A. 1903

MADONNA AT THE POKER NIGHT: PICTORIAL ELEMENTS IN TENNESSEE WILLIAMS' *A STREETCAR NAMED DESIRE*

Despite the fact that many of his finest works *(The Glass Menagerie, Summer and Smoke)* contain striking visual effects, previous criticism has neglected the importance of pictorial elements in the work of Tennessee Williams.At the conclusion of his *Memoirs* (1975), Williams points directly at the power and concreteness of which the visual artist (as opposed to the literary) is capable:

> The work of a fine painter, committed only to vision, abstract and allusive as he pleases, is better able to create for you his moments of intensely perceptive being ... Van Gogh could capture for you moments of beauty, indescribable as descent into madness.[1]

The above statement is revealing not only with regard to Williams' attitude towards the pictorial arts, but also illuminates a process he actually employs with great success in his own study of a "descent into madness," *A Streetcar Named Desire* (1947).

The present paper will consider three aspects of Williams' use of pictorial elements in *A Streetcar Named Desire*: his reference to a specific painting in the stage directions to the third scene of the play, the play's colour symbolism, and the importance of various objects which correspond to signs and symbols frequently found in Renaissance painting.

It is significant that Williams' original title for *Streetcar* was *"The Poker Night,"*[2] and that the title was based on a reference to a painting by Vincent van Gogh, *All Night Café* (1888), in the third scene of the play:

> There is a picture of Van Gogh's of a billiard parlour at night. The kitchen now suggests that sort of lurid nocturnal brilliance, the raw colors of childhood's spectrum. Over the yellow linoleum of the kitchen hangs an electric bulb with a vivid green glass shade. The parlour players ... wear colored shirts, solid blues, a purple, a red-and-white check, a light green, and they are men at the peak of their physical manhood, as coarse and direct as the primary colors. There are vivid slices of watermelon on the table, whiskey bottles, and glasses.[3]

It is obvious from William's description of "The Poker Night" scene that he has taken great pains over the precise visual effects down to the smallest details of colour and shape. Not only does Williams derive the setting of this scene from van Gogh's work, he even forces his audience to view it in pictorial terms as a *tableau vivant,* adding the stage direction, "For a moment there is an absorbed silence as a hand is dealt" (p. 143).

The resemblance between Williams' detailed stage directions and van Gogh's painting would hardly be worth mentioning were it not for the fact that in "The Poker Night" scene, Williams is concerned not only with external but with internal equivalence. The work, which has been called van Gogh's "most expressionist painting"[4] is dominated by colour contrasts, "color suggesting some emotion of an ardent temperament."[5] Specifically, the canvas is marked by the contrasts of the blood red walls and yellow floor with dark green, coffin-shaped billiard table set diagonally in the middle, casting an ominous shadow. The eerieness of the scene is further conveyed by the figure of the landlord in his white coat who faces the viewer from behind the table, and especially by the four luminous lamps suspended from the ceiling, which are surrounded by areas of intensely vibrating yellow light. Perhaps the most interesting comment about this painting was made by van Gogh himself in a letter to his brother Theo:

> I have tried to express the idea that the café is a place where one can ruin oneself, go mad, or commit a crime. So I have tried to express, as it were, the powers of darkness in a low public house, by soft, Louis XV green and malachite, contrasting with yellow-green and harsh blue-greens, and all this in an atmosphere like a devil's furnace, of pale sulphur. And all with an appearance of Japanese gaiety, and the good nature of Tartarin.[6]

Van Gogh's comments about this hallucinating work are extremely revealing when applied to *Streetcar*. Williams too uses striking colour contrasts in this scene ("the raw colors of childhood's spectrum") to create an atmosphere teeming with potential violence in the men "at the peak of their physical manhood" who are as "coarse and direct as the primary colors."

The scene (which significantly begins with the words, "anything wild this deal?") moves from the atmosphere of potential violence to the real thing, and climaxes in Stanley Kowalski's hurling a radio out of the window, striking his wife Stella, and being forcibly restrained from doing further damage to her by the other poker players who grapple with him and finally throw him into a cold shower. The scene concludes with a passionate reconciliation between Stanley and Stella in which he "throws back his head like a baying hound and bellows his wife's name" before they "come together with low animal moans" (p. 154).

Williams creates an atmosphere of barbaric, jungle-like violence in twentieth-century America in which Blanche Dubois (who has come to stay with her sister as a refuge) is first lost and mystified, then trapped and destroyed. As she says to Stella of Stanley and the poker night:

> Thousands and thousands of years have passed him right by, and there he is - Stanley Kowalski - survivor of the Stone Age! Bearing the raw meat home from the kill in the jungle! ...

> Night falls and other apes gather! There in front of the cave, all grunting like him, and swilling and gnawing and hulking! His poker night! - you call - this party of apes! (p. 163)

To create the savage and primitive atmosphere, the playwright employs the harsh primary colours of the jungle where "one can ruin oneself, go mad, or commit a crime."

But Williams not only uses such detailed colour symbolism in this scene avowedly based on van Gogh's painting, he uses it throughout the play as a means of articulating the struggle between the play's two antagonists, Blanche Dubois and Stanley Kowalski; a struggle which ultimately leads to violent rape and Blanche's mental breakdown.

The central conflict in the play may be seen as dramatized through the use of colour. Although in Scene Two Blanche coyly indicates to Stanley that she "likes an artist who paints in strong, bold colors, primary colors" (p. 137), it is her antagonist who is associated with these colours throughout the play: in the opening moments when he returns home bearing "a red-stained package from a butcher's;" the "gaudy pajamas" that lie across the threshold of the bathroom in Scene Four; his green and scarlet silk bowling shirt, which he wears in Scene Five (and which is worn again at the beginning of the rape scene); and in the brilliantly coloured pajama top he waves as a flag before his assault on Blanche.

Even when not actually wearing these articles of clothing, Stanley's speech reinforces the visual connection between himself and bright harsh colours. His pet name for sexual intercourse, for example, is to "get the colored lights going," and the evening of his rape of Blanche he calls "a red-letter night" for both of us.[7] In his description of Stanley in the stage directions, the playwright himself refers to him as "a richly feathered male bird" and "gaudy seed bearer," (p. 128).

Blanche, as her name suggests, is primarily identified (in contrast to Stanley's loud colours) with white, stressing her essential purity, even innocence in the jungle-like world into which she has come as a stranger seeking refuge. Even the first words spoken to her "What's the matter honey? Are you lost?" suggest Blanche's singularity as she arrives in her "white suit with fluffy bodice, necklace and earrings of pearl, white gloves and hat" (p. 117).

In view of the associations made between Blanche and whiteness, it is interesting to note that in the "Poker Night" scene, Stanley throws "a small white radio" which Blanche is listening to out of the window, thus prefiguring - by means of colour - the play's conclusion, when Blanche herself is thrown out of the house by Stanley.

Of course, in view of Blanche's promiscuity (her visit to her sister in New Orleans has been precipitated by her being run out of Laurel, Mississippi), it is possible to view Blanche's identification with white as an ironic use of colour by the author. Ruby Cohn, for example, has seen Blanche's translation of her own name

"White woods. Like an orchard in spring," as a fantasy, suggesting that "the purity of Blanche-white is undermined by the thicket of Du Bois-woods. "Anglicized, Blanche's name is Du Boys, and under her chaste surface, Blanche lusts for boys."[8]

In addition, soon after her arrival, Blanche changes into a red satin robe which she uses to flirt with Stanley, and which she also wears briefly in the play's final scene.

This apparent inconsistency in Williams' use of colour symbolism is justified by Blanche's own nature, which contains both innocence and promiscuity, the latter a result of the shattered dreams of her youth. As Stella observes, "When she was young, very young, she had an experience that - killed her illusions" (p. 189). However, the essential division in Blanche's character is ultimately resolved by the playwright in the final scene of the play, and, once again, this resolution is indicated to the audience by means of a symbolic use of colour.

When Blanche comes on stage in the final scene, she is wearing her red satin robe, suggestive both in colour and material of Stanley's forced sexual possession of her in the previous scene. As she prepares to leave the house, however, she changes her clothes, and the colour of her new outfit is specifically remarked upon by the other characters.

> Eunice: What a pretty blue jacket.
> Stella: It's lilac colored.
> Blanche: You're both mistaken. It's Della Robbia blue. The blue of the robe in the old Madonna pictures (p. 219).

Although Blanche is clearly suffering from complete nervous collapse at this point in the play, the associations between herself and the blue traditionally associated with the Virgin in Renaissance art is by no means an accident. Rather, it is fully consistent with the direction of Williams' symbolism from early on in the play. In the second scene, for example, Blanche sings the following in the bathroom:

> 'From the land of sky-blue water, They brought a captive maid!' (p. 132)

This song stresses the connection between Blanche, the colour blue, the forced captivity of an innocent maid, and obviously foreshadows the ending of the play when, dressed in blue, she is literally taken captive by the Doctor and Nurse, and led out of the house ... "a captive maid!" This change of costume from red satin to blue, at the end of the play, obliges us to see Blanche as casting off her sensual side in favour of a new innocence, with strong implications of spiritual rebirth.

Although the analogy between Blanche and the Virgin Mary suggested by Williams' colour symbolism seems strange, it is fully in keeping with numerous references found throughout the play which reveal that, in his representation of Blanche Du Bois as a tragic heroine, Williams was thinking of attributes traditionally identified with the Virgin in Renaissance art.

In Scene Ten, for example, Blanche wears a rhinestone tiara, a crumpled white satin gown, and a pair of scuffed silver slippers with brilliants set in their heels. Even though Stanley scoffs at Blanche's terrible predicament: "And with that crazy crown on! What queen do you think you are!", the image of Blanche at her most pitiful may be seen as a variation on the familiar image of Mary as Queen of Heaven, portrayed with a crown bearing the twelve stars of the apocalyptic vision (Revelation 12:9). Stanley's sarcastic reference to Blanche as a "queen" is, in fact, taken seriously by the dramatist.

In the following scene, following her rape by Stanley, Blanche appears in the amber light of the doorway. The stage directions refer to her "tragic radiance" and to the "sculptural lines of her body." Ruby Cohn has objected that this scene "borders on sentimentality ... aggravated by such pretentious stage directions,"[9] but if we realize that Williams is trying to create the visual image of the aureole frequently used in pictorial representations of the Blessed Virgin, consisting "of a field of radiance and splendour which encircles the whole body and appears to emerge from it. In some cases the aureole follows the form of the body and clings closely to it, appearing as a fringe of light," the stage directions become more comprehensible.[10]

Williams not only uses colour and light to suggest an analogy between Blanche and the Virgin Mary, but numerous other indications as well. Her astrological sign, - in contrast to Stanley's Capricorn, the goat - is Virgo, and she is ironically referred to by him as a "lily," a flower suggestive of death (and picked up later in the old Mexican woman's cry, "Flores para los muertos") but also traditionally symbolizing the purity of the Virgin amid the sins of this world.

In addition, in the final scene Blanche holds a "silver-backed mirror" (p. 218) reminiscent of the spotless mirror which is one of the attributes of the Virgin. Williams' explicit stage directions informing the reader that her look is of "sorrowful perplexity as though all human experience shows on her face" reminds one of another devotional representation of Mary, that of the *Mater Dolorosa*. The Cathedral bells which chime during the scene and the fact that, when Stanley orders the Doctor and Matron to remove Blanche by force, Pablo cries, "Madre de Dios! Cosa mala, muy, muy mala" are further indications of Williams' intentions in this scene.[11]

Perhaps the most persuasive piece of visual evidence indicating the religious symbolism underlying the final scene of *Streetcar* is Williams' manipulation of Stella's child. Unlike Esther Merle Jackson, who states that the playwright "exposes [Blanche's] progress toward the last circle of hell," I would argue that to see the last scene only in terms of Blanche's fall is to miss Williams' true intention which is to suggest not "the ultimate point of descent"[12] but to indicate that Blanche's tragic destruction on one level, may be seen as heroic transcendence on another. It is for this reason that Scene Eleven is filled with imagery suggesting not merely death, but rebirth as well.

Stella's baby, born at approximately the same time as Blanche's violation by Stanley in the previous scene, is associated with Blanche in the final moment of the play. As Blanche leaves followed by the Doctor and the Matron, Stella cries out "Blanche! Blanche, Blanche!" Her cry is of course not answered in words, but the visual action suggests a kind of response to her cry; "(Eunice descends to Stella and places the child in her arms. It is wrapped in a pale blue blanket. Stella accepts the child, sobbingly.)" By giving her the child in answer to her plea for Blanche who is leaving, and by having the child wrapped in a *pale blue blanket,* a colour we have come to associate with Blanche, Williams clearly suggests an identification between the tragic fall of one and the birth of the other. In the light of Williams' colour symbolism throughout the play, this exchange may be seen as a suggestion that Blanche's symbolic death has ultimately resulted in new life.

This connection between death and rebirth, so essential to Christian doctrine, is further conveyed by the fact that the baby's birth is celebrated by a bunch of grapes, a traditional symbol for the blood of Christ and the wine of the Holy Communion, and these grapes are immediately associated in the mind of Blanche with her own death:

> You know what I shall die of? (She plucks a grape.) I shall die of eating an unwashed grape one day out on the ocean ... 'Poor lady,' they'll say, 'the quinine did her no good. That unwashed grape has transported her soul to heaven' (p. 220).

Thus Blanche's fall, prefigured at the very outset of the play when she describes her journey ("They told me to take a streetcar named Desire, and then transfer to one called Cemeteries and ride six blocks and get off at Elysian Fields!") is actually part of a process which goes beyond death and hints at something like heroic transcendence, which is conveyed in the measured tones of Blanche's final words, "Whoever you are - I have always depended on the kindness of strangers," so full of tragic irony for the sister who has consented to her removal.

Through a careful examination of the play's pictorial elements, it has become clear that the end of this play is not so much a "descent into hell" as an expression of spiritual purification through suffering.

University of Leiden — Henry I. Schvey

NOTES

1 Tennessee Williams, *Memoirs* (Garden City, New York: Doubleday, 1975), p. 316.

2 Williams, "On a Streetcar Named Success," in *where I Live: Selected Essays* (New York: New Directions, 1978), p. 19.

3 Tennessee Williams, *A Streetcar Named Desire* (Harmondsworth: Penguin Books, 1975), p. 143. Subsequent references will be

to this edition.

4 Lara Vinca Masina, *Van Gogh: The Life and Work of the Artist*, trans. Caroline Beamish (London: Thame and Hudson, 1967) p. 29.

5 Vincent van Gogh, *The Complete Letters of Vincent van Gogh* (Greenwich, Connecticut: New York Graphic Society, 1958), p. 29.

6 Van Gogh, p. 31.

7 *Streetcar*, pp. 196, 199, 211. Although beyond the scope of this paper, it is clear that the playwright also uses light as a means of contrasting the characters of Stanley and Blanche. The former associates light with sexual activity (the "coloured lights" and the effect that on his wedding night he smashes all the light bulbs with Stella's slipper), while Blanche is terrified of the light; "And turn that over-light off! ... I won't be looked at in this merciless glare" (p. 120). At the end of the play, Stanley's "victory" is expressed through his tearing Blanche's paper lantern off the light bulb and handing it to her. "She cries as if the lantern was herself" (p. 223).

8 Ruby Cohn, "The Garrulous Grotesques of Tennessee Williams," in Tennessee Williams: *A Collection of Critical Essays*, ed. Stephen S. Stanton (Englewood Cliffs, New Jersey: Prentice Hall, 1977), p. 46.

9 Cohn, p. 51.

10 George Ferguson, *Signs and Symbols in Christian Art* (New York: Oxford University Press, 1977), p. 148.

11 *Streetcar*, p. 224. This exchange is not included in American editions of the play.

12 Esther Merle Jackson, "The Anti-Hero in the Plays of Tennessee Williams," in *Tennessee Williams: A Collection of Critical Essays*, p. 95.

STYRON'S CASE AND "SOPHIE'S CHOICE"

The novels of William Styron have proved both compelling and embarrassing. All literary markers seem to point in the opposite direction from his approach to the novel, but we read him avidly, only to turn upon him afterwards for having enthralled us by illegitimate means. He is, as everyone knows, the author of the grand theme, the large subject carefully "researched," whereas the more representative interest of the modern American novel has focussed on the individual's tenuous, often abrasive relation with a limiting, imprisoning environment. And while everyone else seems to be neurotically self-conscious about the possibilities of form and language for the novel in our time, Styron uses well-tried, timeworn conventions of the Southern romance. He simply continues where his literary forbears, William Faulkner, Robert Penn Warren, Thomas Wolfe and F. Scott Fitzgerald left off. It is not that he is impervious to the literary situation; on the contrary, he has been sensitive to criticism and ambitious for literary success. As a matter of fact, his erstwhile friend and lifelong rival Norman Mailer early accused him of literary log-rolling.[1] It is rather that nothing has convinced him to abandon his conception of the novel, and he puts the burden on us to prove him wrong.

In reading Styron's new novel, *Sophie's Choice* (1979), we are made to ponder his literary career, for one thing because his narrator, nicknamed Stingo (earlier prep-school Stinky), whose surname follows on the heels alphabetically, of "Strohmyer" and "Stutz,"[2] is the author fictionalized. The degree of fictionalization increases with the distance in time. When the narrator returns to "those faraway afternoons of First Novelhood" (p. 112) in 1947, he is a fictional re-creation invoked, ironically and at times affectionately, by William Styron in his early fifties; in 1947 Stingo was passionately engaged in the writing of *Inheritance of Night* (read *Lie Down in Darkness*), a twenty-two-year-old innocent from Virginia come to Manhattan and soon after to Brooklyn to confront the European experience of Sophie Zawistowska, a Polish Roman Catholic survivor of Auschwitz. The closer the narrator approaches the present time of the writing of "*Sophie's Choice,* which itself is part of the subject-matter of the novel, the more straightforwardly informative, and didactic, his voice becomes. To be alive to the tone of the narrative is to be aware of the fallibility, the "staggeringly puerile inexperience" (p. 203) of twenty-two-year-old Stingo, "a gullible and simple-minded waif" (p. 432) from the

South among the Jews of Brooklyn. During the summer of 1947 he is initiated into the mysteries and perplexities of sex and of death, the two subjects, incidentally, upon which his own "most memorable dreams" turn (p. 45). Again and again he proves inadequate to the experience; and Stingo/Styron in middle age comes to write Sophie's story, as Sophie herself had wanted to write a novel about Auschwitz, partly to lay the ghost of his own past guilt.

In 1947 Stingo's youth is "at its lowest ebb" (p. 3). He had left the Marine Corps two years earlier, too young to have seen actual combat, this in contrast to his experienced friend Jack Brown who lost a leg on Iwo Jima; the ghastliness of recent history has passed Stingo by. He reads lousy manuscripts at McGraw-Hill levelling at them the scorn that could only have been mustered by "one who had just finished reading *Seven Types of Ambiguity*" (p. 5). Indeed, in the evening hours, Stingo reads all the right literary texts, and hoards the prologue to a novel readied to preface the experience he still lacks. It is heavily indebted in tone to the opening passages of *All The King's Men,* but his own words bowl him over at every rereading. The experience soon reaches him in a letter from his father announcing the suicide by leaping from the window of a Manhattan building, of his hometown flame, Maria Hunt, but it is only days later, when the shock has worn off, that he recognizes its potential for his novel:

> Again and again I pored over the newspaper clipping my father had sent, becoming warm with excitement as the awareness grew that Maria and her family might serve as the exemplary figures for the novel's cast of characters. The rather desperate wreck of a father, a chronic lush and also something of a womanizer; the mother, slightly unbalanced and a grim pietist, known throughout the upper-middle-class, country-club and high-Episcopal echelons of the city for her long-suffering tolerance of her husband's mistress, herself a social-climbing dimwit from the sticks; and the daughter finally, poor dead Maria, doomed and a victim from the outset through all the tangled misunderstandings, bourgeois family life the closest thing to hell on earth - my God, I thought, it was perfectly marvelous, a gift from the sky! (p. 111)

This description, of course, closely approximates the characters in *Lie Down in Darkness* (1951), the novel that made Styron famous at twenty-six. But characters alone do not make a novel, and Stingo himself must first be driven to suicidal despair by living through the degradation and death of Sophie, who so resembles Maria, before he can fully dramatize the plight of his heroine.

Already now, too, Nat Turner casts a shadow. "I'm going to make a *book* out of that slave," Stingo tells his friend, Sophie's Jewish lover, Nathan Landau. Styron is by turns outrageous, sly and defensive about *The Confessions of Nat Turner*. It is of course the novel that is freshest in everybody's mind, including the author's, as are the attacks on it by militant blacks and some whites. Its theme of slavery in the American South increasingly insinuates itself into the texture of *Sophie's Choice* as a muted parallel to the total enslavement in the Nazi deathcamps. So Nat Turner also will have to be exorcised, but first Stingo has to deal with his "beloved and bedeviled bourgeois New South family whose every move and gesture, I had begun to realize were played out in the presence of a vast, brooding company of black witnesses, all sprung from the loins of bondage" (pp. 420-1). Stingo cannot elude the "fearsome and ungodly history" (p. 72) of his native ground; indeed the events of 1947 throw that history into high perspective.

As with most Styron characters, dreams play an important part in Stingo's life. They are never as mysterious and imaginatively satisfying as Nat Turner's recurring dream of "the strange building standing so lonely and remote upon its ocean promontory,"[3] but they do help to bring out more clearly certain submerged significances. As Maria tends to merge with Sophie in Stingo's imagination, so does Nat Turner fuse into a dream about another Negro slave, Artiste, and thereby passes into Stingo's family history, even as Stingo in the end is admitted to the dead bodies of Sophie and Nathan as "a member of the family" (p. 507). For by a curious and intriguing twist that is the very stuff of fiction, the money that Stingo's great-grandfather made from the sale of his slave Artiste into the hell of the turpentine forests of Georgia pays for Stingo's keep in the "Pink Palace," Yetta Zimmerman's "Liberty Hall," the rambling roominghouse in the Flatbush part of Brooklyn where, after leaving McGraw-Hill, he spends the summer in close companionship with Sophie and Nathan. In later years that money will haunt him, but by then he has made a packet on another slave. "What the hell, once a racist exploiter always a racist exploiter" (pp. 32-3) - Styron tries to needle his detractors still. Also, the peanut farm in Southampton County, scene of Nat Turner's insurrection, that Stingo's father offers to his son as a haven away from the "barbarity" (p. 188) of New York City, the father inherited from a bachelor friend, who was also a rabid racist, "10 miles to the right of Mussolini" (p. 107). That farm is the scene of the following daydream:

> In my mind's prism the years like blue hills rolled peacefully away toward the horizon of the far future. *Inheritance of Night* a remarkable success, gaining laurels rarely shed upon the work of a writer so young. A short novel then, also acclaimed, having to do with my wartime experiences - a taut, searing book eviscerating the military in a tragicomedy of the absurd. Meanwhile, Sophie and I living on the modest plantation in dignified seclusion, my reputation growing, the author himself being increasingly importuned by the media but steadfastly refusing all interviews. "I just farm peanuts," says he, going about his work. At age thirty or thereabouts another masterpiece, *These Blazing Leaves,* the chronicle of that tragic Negro firebrand Nat Turner (p. 450).

Conspicuously lacking here is mention of Styron's longest novel - as long, that is, as *Sophie's Choice* - *Set This House on Fire* (1960), a Gothic tale of sexual perversion, rape and murder, set mostly in Italy, that was remaindered in hardbound within a year of publication. Styron himself has expressed affection for parts of it, but it is also the only novel where very significant cuts were made in the proofs;[4] this is remarkable for a writer who works slowly, but usually has done with a novel once he has put it into the hands of his publisher. Several reviewers noticed the omission of Styron's Italian novel, and one of them expressed surprise that the author of *Set This House on Fire* should have written *Sophie's Choice*.[5] In reply it might be argued that *Sophie's Choice* is Styron's rewriting of the earlier novel.

Set This House on Fire has been criticised for two defects especially: its deficient structure and its fortuitous ending. Whether or not one wants to argue for a special relation between the two novels, one can proffer a comparative judgement to the effect that both structure and ending are better managed in *Sophie's Choice*. For one thing, Stingo is a more personable narrator, who must indeed soon share the limelight with Sophie as her story moves to the centre, but who is not relegated to near insignificance, as is Peter Leverett in *Set This House on Fire*. Stingo is given the advantage of the long perspective, whereas Peter is still rather naive when, at a remove of only two years, he tries to reconstruct the macabre events in Sambuco. So Cass Kinsolving comes to dominate the story - to such an extent that one critic has seen him as a continuation of Peter Leverett and a more mature autobiographical projection of the author.[6] Peter is a colourless Nick Carraway; "you look so *ordinary*," Cass's ingenuous wife tells him at first meeting, and his friend from prep-school, Mason Flagg, addresses him as: "Squarest of the Square."[7] So it does not surprise us that Cass finally speaks the words that ought by rights to have been Peter's:

> And I kept thinking of the new sun coming up over the coast of Virginia and the Carolinas, and how it must have looked from those galleons, centuries ago, when after black night, dawn broke like a trumpet blast, and there it was, immense and green and glistening against the crashing sees. And suddenly I wanted more than anything in my life to go back there. And I knew I would go ... (*Set This House on Fire*, p. 500)

Shades of "the matchless *Gatsby*."[8]

At the close of *Sophie's Choice,* Sophie and Nathan, decked out in theatrical garb, are stretched out on Sophie's bed, their love couch, a double suicide. If for a moment, for the sake of argument and much too schematically, we identify Sophie with Cass and Nathan with Mason in the triangles formed with Stingo and Peter, the pat parallelism is disfigured by Cass's ultimate affirmation. And then we remember that, not only had Cass, like Sophie, been frequently suicidal, there had been moments when he had felt an urge to blot out his family as well; but, for all the rhetoric of doom, Sophie might have described Cass's plight, unkindly, as "undeserved unhappiness" (p. 130). Indeed, today's reader may well conclude that in *Set This House on Fire* Styron's rhetoric is in excess of the suffering of his characters. This is equally true for the novella *The Long March* (1953), which some readers, in disparagement of the novels, have tried to promote too generously to Styron's *Seize the Day*. It does not hold for *Sophie's Choice*, be it that one wants to challenge the viability of Styron's rhetoric altogether. This is a question we shall let rest till later.

It may be instructive to juxtapose a few passages:

> ... as we zoomed toward the far green reaches of the island he talked his head off, and with a sorcerer's charm. Jokes tumbled from his lips, and witty wicked allusions, and airy ballooning puns; his spoofery was a marvel, so wild and preposterous that Celia, rosy with laughter, had to implore him to stop, put her head down in his lap and cried, "Stop! *Stop it!*" while I collapsed in merriment among the wrenches. (*Set This House on Fire*, p. 159)

> We walked in the gayest of spirits toward the subway station - Sophie between us now, her arms linked in ours - and he returned to that grits-and-molasses accent he rendered with such fantastic precision; there was no sarcasm this time, no intent to needle me, and his intonation, accurate enough to fool a native of Memphis or Mobile, caused me to nearly choke with laughter. But his gift was not mimicry alone; what emanated from him so drolly was the product of dazzling invention (p. 75).

It is indeed the resemblance between Mason Flagg and Nathan Landau, both brilliant and self-educated, and both masters of make-believe, that is most striking.[9] Petèr finds Mason immensely attractive" (*Set This House on Fire*, p. 63), and Stingo is beguiled by Nathan's "devastating attractiveness" (p. 416). Both Stingo and Peter long try to stave off the awareness of the darker side of their delightful friends. It is the minor characters who bring it out into the open: Maggie, who calls Mason "a *monster*" (p. 231), a name also, and with similar emphasis, applied to Nathan by Morris Fink, a part-time janitor at the Pink Palace (p. 60). Or consider the following passage:

> Once more she was silent, but now I felt a tremor run through her body. "He scares me when he hits me like that." Her lips were trembling and I held her very close against my side, as I would a little girl. "But that's all right," she blurted out suddenly. "I'm mad for him," just positively *mad* for him!"

This could have been Sophie to Stingo about Nathan, but it is actually Celia to Peter about Mason (*Set This House on Fire*, p. 165). In the end Celia can take charge of her own fate and go to Reno, but Sophie's doom was sealed even before she knew Nathan.

The two novels have the same literary progenitor, Thomas Wolfe. In *Set This House on Fire* his influence was particularly felt in Cass Kinsolving's hyperbolic monologues. As *Sophie's Choice* is a writer's book with frequent references to the literary world, Wolfe can be introduced by name. He is first mentioned in the opening pages when Stingo relates how his fortunes at McGraw-Hill began to decline with the arrival of a new editor in chief, "whom I secretly called the Weasel - a near-anagram of his actual surname" (p. 15). The Weasel, he tells us, was Wolfe's second editor. (An anagram, then, of Edward Aswell;[10] no doubt we are encouraged to remember Wolfe's own portrait of "the fox" in *You Can't Go Home Again,* a take-off on his first editor, Maxwell Perkins.) Stingo utterly fails to make contact with the Weasel, "a cold company man" (p. 16), and that is unfortunate because "I would have given all I had to spend a chummy, relaxed evening with a man like the Weasel, pumping him for fresh new anecdotes about the master" (p. 30).[11] Wolfe has other admirers. Stingo's mother had been "a devoted fan long before I had read a word of Wolfe," and we come upon her, racked by cancer, seeking oblivion from her pain in *You Can't Go Home Again*. And Sophie, after her arrival in the United States making up for lost time, read Dos Passos, Hemingway and Dreiser, but it was *Of Time and the River* that "excited her the most of all the books she read that winter and spring," before she met Stingo. But the name of Wolfe also occurs in connection with Auschwitz. Its commandant, Rudolf Höss, is born in the same year and under the same sign as Wolfe (p. 149), and, irony of the time relation,Sophie meets Höss for the first time, Stingo tells us, on "the birthday of three of my heroes: of my father, of the autumn-haunted Thomas Wolfe, and of wild Nat Turner, that fanatical black demon whose ghost had seared my imagination throughout my boyhood and youth" (p. 220).

Both tales are told as detective stories. In *Set This House on Fire* the question at stake is actually the resolution of a murder, but when we finally learn who did it, we feel keen disappointment because the village half-wit Valerio does not meet the measure of our imagination; he is simply sprung upon us by the author. The choice offered Sophie is as vile as any murder, "in the realm of the unspeakable" (p. 365), and she can work herself up to the revelation of it, the speaking of it, only towards the end of her tale. Peter was actually in Sambuco when the murder took place which is described at the end of the first part of the novel. In the second part he recollects those wild Italian days in tranquillity, from a distance, and, with the help of Cass Kinsolving, a much more perceptive participant more deeply involved in the outlandish events, establishes the truth of the latter's guilt. Stingo was not present at the scene of Sophie's choice; what indeed appals him is the time relation: "on that afternoon, as Sophie first set foot on the railroad platform in Auschwitz, it was a lovely spring morning in Raleigh, North Carolina, where I was gorging myself on bananas" (p. 217); Stingo was trying to satisfy the minimum weight requirement for entrance into the Marine Corps, like other young innocents - remember Studs Lonigan and his friends? - before him.

Whereas Cass's voice takes over much of the second half of *Set This House on Fire,* Stingo tells most of Sophie's story himself. Judging from the moments he hands the tale over to Sophie, this was a wise decision. Sophie was raised bilingual in Polish and German and has a good knowledge of French; her English is not bad at all, but the shape of her sentences is monotonous and her idiom distracting. Of course Stingo/Styron is aware of the problem; he had faced a similar one when he decided to tell Nat Turner's story in the first person. His solution then drew much criticism - undeservedly on the face of it, if one considers that the author gave the best language only sparingly to try to duplicate "the delicious inaccuracies of Sophie's English" (p. 51).

Styron is very skillful at structuring his narrative: interweaving the stories of Stingo and Sophie, managing the frequent timeshifts and changes of scene, and highlighting the cruel ironies of the time relation. "What's Owswitch?" (p. 213), asks Stingo's impervious, Jewish fellow lodger, Morris Fink. The question remains unanswerable - "no one will ever understand Auschwitz" (p. 513) - but blatant ignorance is criminal. So Stingo will help demonstrate how *"absolute evil is never extinguished from the world"* (p. 513) by writing about Sophie's life and death. But the language he has chosen for the story is different shades of Southern purple and that creates a measure of embarrassment. It is a language that never lets go of the reader, that will not trust to understatement, and, in its metaphors, will plump for clichés rather than for the original image that might slow the reader down. It delights in sound effects and in dictionary words like "mucilaginous" (p. 168), "paludal" (p. 188), "matutinal" (pp. 257,498), "luminiferous" (p. 302) and "unguentary" (p. 457); "parturition" (p. 215), "tintinnabulation" (p. 226), "famishment" (p. 319) and "depredation" (p. 349); and, of course, the Faulknerian "immemorial," "perdurable," etc. Emotions are described as physical sensations, most characteristically the sensation of choking - "despair over her loss encircled my throat like hands" (p. 318) - but other expressions of physical outrage as well: "anguish similar to that of being buried alive under a ton of cinders" (p. 291); "a pain of nostalgia so intense that it was like being impaled upon a spear" (p. 421). And we might as well face the worst (Stingo has just made some rash remarks): "I now saw that I could not have caused her worse pain had she possessed a hot inflamed cicatrix from which I had savagely yanked the stitches in a horrible ball of fresh sutures and outraged flesh" (p. 308).

These instances are not cited to dismiss Styron. Although they are not always seamlessly embedded in their context, the reader stumbles less frequently than listing them in isolation would suggest. Styron is, of course, aware of the pitfalls of the literary tradition he follows. When Nathan really wants to get at Stingo he says: "You have a pretty snappy talent in the traditional Southern mode. But you also have all the old clichés" (p. 208). This is meant to hurt - it is indeed a far cry from Nathan's earlier extravagant praise - but especially because it applies to Stingo/Styron's first novel, it is not entirely unjust. For some readers *Lie Down in Darkness* is still the first novel that never dies, and that has never been equalled. Rereading it today one is still impressed by the skillful structure and the created sense of place, but the pervasive impression is of precocity rather than of lived experience; the emotional and intellectual life does not quite fill out the potentialities of the mastered form. One way of illustrating the point is to consider Faulkner's influence. It has been remarked upon from the very beginning, could indeed hardly have been missed, and starting with Malcolm Cowley,[12] readers have maintained that Styron borrowed Faulknerian techniques and situations but transformed them for his own ends. This is not the effect on the reader today; when he comes to Peyton's interior monologue he forgets about Styron and is overcome by his *memory* of Faulkner, because Peyton's plight, in contrast to Sophie's, has not been made sufficiently challenging to appropriate the means of its portrayal.

At this point one may tentatively propose a rough distinction between *Lie Down in Darkness* and *Set This House on Fire* as novels that deal with literary situations, and *The Confessions of Nat Turner* and *Sophie's Choice* that tackle historical, or public themes. Now, it is arguable that clichés of language are more easily absorbed by the texture of "public" novels than of "literary" novels, possibly because the printed texts closest to the "public" novel deal with history and society and are non-literary. This differentiation may also apply to clichés of situation. If readers of *The Confessions of Nat Turner*, for instance, complain that Nat's passion for white Margaret is a cliché, they mean something different from the objection that Milton Loftis in *Lie Down in Darkness* is a cliché of a Southern gentleman. The first objection refers primarily to a social stereotype - it does not immediately suggest comparison with the fiction of, say, Richard Wright or Ralph Ellison - whereas the second refers us to the Southern literary tradition. Again, it may be easier to bring the social stereotype to literary life because the writer dramatizes a notion rather than reflects a literary practice.

Stingo's experiences fit more snugly in the mould of the "literary" novel, Sophie's of the "public" novel, and the distance between the two is bridged by the voice of the narrator. Stingo's main preoccupation during the summer of 1947 is his obdurate virginity, and his inspiration as the teller of that tale is Philip Roth. In his twenty-second year, "the most anxiety-filled of all" (p. 438), he is "the prey of an ever-unfulfilled randiness" (p. 348). Sophie, meanwhile, is tortured by a survivor's guilt, and in order to delve down to the sources of that guilt Styron read widely about the concentration camps, and was most particularly struck by Richard L. Rubenstein's *The Cunning of History* (1975). Indeed, Rubenstein's book stands in the same relation to *Sophie's Choice* as Stanley Elkin's *Slavery* does to *The Confessions of Nat Turner*. Styron elaborates on this in a passionate endorsement of Rubenstein's argument in an article, "Hell Reconsidered," published a year before the appearance of the novel.[13] The article augured ill for the novel because Styron had written it with the proselytizing zeal of the converted; one was not looking forward to another rumpus about a Styron novel, this time under attack by outraged Jews.

As a matter of fact, Rubenstein's book has proved particularly useful for the novel. It is central to Rubenstein's argument that Auschwitz was both a slave camp and an extermination camp, and constituted a "society of total domination" of both Jews and Gentiles based on the simple but "absolute *expendability* of human life" (p. 235). Stingo, who has noticed the tattooed number on her wrist, is surprised to learn that Sophie is not Jewish. This is of the essence of the tale that she unfolds, because her guilt turns out to be that not only of the survivor but, to some extent, of the accomplice. Sophie and Stingo are fellow Gentiles self-exiled among the Jews in Brooklyn. He becomes her confidant, which her Jewish lover, obsessed with the Holocaust, can never be, because they hail from similar backgrounds. Poland conjures up images of the American South - "or at least the South of other, not-so-distant times;" like the Old South it was tormented into its shape "out of adversity, penury and defeat," and the "sinister zone of likeness" between the two has to do with the matter of race (p. 247). While Sophie has to live with memories of "a nation which practically invented anti-Semitism" (p. 472), Stingo is heir to a region that breeds racist politicians like Senator Theodore Gilmore Bilbo and that mutilates and lynches Bobby Weed.

"Like numerous Southerners of a certain background, learning and sensibility, I have from the beginning responded warmly to Jews," Stingo tells us; indeed he has to conclude that "an unconscious urge to be among Jews" had been at least part of his reason for coming to Brooklyn (p. 39). In his hometown in Virginia the Jews had been an integral part of the social world; only their religious and domestic lives had seemed mysterious to him.

> It was out of the glare of daylight and the bustle of business, when Jews disappeared into their domestic quarantine and the seclusion of their sinister and Asiatic worship - with its cloudy suspicion of incense and rams' horns and sacrificial offerings, tambourines and veiled women, lugubrious anthems and keening banshee wails in a dead language - that the trouble began for the eleven-year-old Presbyterian (p. 162).

But, then, the mind of eleven-year-old Stingo had been full of extraordinarily charged images - of sexual intercourse, for instance, which he had visualized as "a brutish art committed in secrecy upon dyed blondes by huge drunken unshaven ex-convicts with their shoes on" (p. 311). It is the gorgeous Leslie Lapidus who will, he hopes, enlighten him on both counts. She turns out to live in thoroughly American opulence, a Cadillac at the front door and a Pissarro (genuine) on the wall, but she puts sex where her mouth is rather than where she ought to. Stingo will only begin to understand her type when he comes to read books like *Goodbye, Columbus*.

Sophie's relation to Jews is of course infinitely more complex and tragic. Her father was a virulently anti-Semitic professor of law at Cracow, "a superconservative in a faculty of right-wingers" (p. 238). Initially Sophie must hide the truth about him, tell lies because the truth that he preached the extermination of the Jews even before the Nazis institutionalized it, is too horrible to endure; and it is only towards the end of her tale, when other horrors have been revealed, that she remakrs: "I sometimes got to think that everything bad on earth, every evil that was ever invented had to do with my father" (p. 466). Styron takes time out for a formal sketch of Professor Zbigniew Biegański:

> He was a tall robust-looking man, usually garbed in a frock coat and a shirt with wing collar and a broad foulard tie. Old-fashioned dress, but not at all grotesque in Poland for that time. His face was classically Polish: high wide cheekbones, blue eyes, rather full lips, the broad nose tilting up, large elfin ears. He wore sideburns and his light fine hair was swept back evenly, always nicely coiffed. A couple of artificial teeth made of silver slightly marred his good looks, but only when he opened his mouth wide. Among his colleagues he was considered something of a dandy, though not absurdly so; his considerable academic reputation was a safeguard against ridicule (p. 238).

The professor is a domestic tyrant who exploits his daughter and despises her. He creates an ambience of "rapturous Germanism" (p. 369), but grafted on a time long past and gone, so that this romantic zealot is cut out to be one of the first victims of "the stainless-steel, jackbooted, mammoth modern power, the first technological state" (p. 250). With him dies his colleague and disciple, Sophie's cold husband Kazik.

The professor is one of Styron's finest characterizations. He was the overwhelming reality of Sophie's formative years, and indeed beyond, and he is brought to full life in the novel. Stingo's father is equally present, a loving portrait that reminds one of Updike's homage to his father in *The Centaur*.[14] For all the guilt of its history, the South has an honourable legacy also - as indeed has Poland as represented in the resistance fighter Wanda - and this legacy is dramatized by Stingo's father with his concern for the past and family, his basic liberalism and his running fight with "the monstrous leviathan known as American business" (p. 108), in particular its lieutenants, "those piratical devils, Washington Duke and his son, 'Buck' Duke" (p. 30). But, above all else, he represents the rurally rooted values of the South vs. the treacherous North, especially that "octopus of a city," New York; "I've never been there, but really it is *possibly* true that, as you wrote me, there are parts of Brooklyn that remind one of *Richmond?*" (p. 291)

South meets North when Stingo's father confronts a Manhattan taxidriver. But the Northerners never get down South, although Stingo, Nathan and Sophie are all excited about a prospective trip to Dixie, with a special excursion to Nat Turner country. In flight from Nathan, Stingo and Sophie do not get beyond

Washington, and when Stingo continues flight on his own, he discovers that the "sprawling concrete blight" of the North has spread south of the "broad Potomac viscid with sewage" and has contaminated his home state. "Was all this not merely Yankee carcinoma, spreading its growth into my beloved Old Dominion?" (p. 504).The South will not shelter him now; he must return to Brooklyn to face the disaster at the end of that summer of 1947.

Doom has hovered over the novel from the very first meeting of Stingo with Sophie and Nathan whose violent lovemaking is followed by Nathan's vociferous attack on Sophie and, when he gets in the way, on Stingo. It is a pattern that will be repeated time and again, and it is Stingo's guilt through inexperience and thoughtlessness that he fails to help forestall the disaster. He has a knack of being distracted when he ought to act decisively. Nathan, in his dark moments, sits in vituperative judgement on his friends' racist heritage, but at other times he can be "utterly, fatally glamorous" (p. 187). He is "the ranting ogre become Prince Charming" (p. 74); there are fleeting moments in which "the attractive and compelling in him seemed in absolute equipoise with the subtly and indefinable sinister" (p. 116). His brother Larry, a physician, is in a position to put it more tersely: "The truth is that my brother's quite mad" (p. 424). For all that, he is a fascinating character, the most interesting Jew in Styron's fiction. Stingo is "quite simply devoted to Nathan" (p. 416) who is something of an older brother to him; Sophie is totally, masochistically in love with Nathan; and the reader can go along with that.

Still the question remains: is Nathan's significance to be limited, ultimately, to that of prompter of Sophie's and Stingo's guilt feelings? Could not Styron have imagined a more meaningful explanation for Nathan's behaviour? He lamely reads into him a prophecy for aftertimes - "his image has always seemed to foreshadow these wretched unending years of madness, illusion, error, dream and strife" (p. 445) - but after Auschwitz, what is so bad about the post-World War II era? Styron never gets beyond the occasional rhethorical reference to "several barbaric American wars" (p. 23). If the resolution of Nathan's case, which is moving as it is, had been sought in the moral rather than in the pathological sphere, it might have been better attuned to the weighty questions the novel poses.

In any novel the author takes a number of calculated risks hoping they will pay off, and in a novel like *Sophie's Choice,* which lives as much by its structure as by its texture, mistakes are especially noticed. The novel's worst mistake occurs in the wake of its most excruciating scene when, on the railroad platform at Auschwitz, a drunken camp doctor offers Sophie a truly satanic choice. The scene is well paced and forcefully narrated, but is immediately followed by a deflating explanation of the doctor's psychology. If there were any doubt that Styron was conscious of taking a risk at such a crucial point in the narrative, we only have to read the first sentence of the chapter that follows his disquisition on the doctor's psyche: "All my life I have retained a streak of uncontrolled didacticism" (p. 489). Indeed, as the protagonist is also the novelist we come across frequent statements of authorial quirks and intentions. On the whole the structure of the novel is very artful, but inevitably the reader will challenge certain decisions. For instance, Stingo's tug of war with Leslie Lapidus is well told and functional, but when much later he has a similar exhausting bout with a girl named Mary Alice Grimball (yes), he might have let it go at his first notebook entry that Mary Alice was "something *worse* than a Cock Tease, a Whack-off artist" (p. 432), for the reader can very well imagine the mores of "that sexually bedeviled era" (p. 120), the nineteen-forties, for himself. Or the theft of Stingo's money: the reader expects it to be meaningful but it turns out to be a mere matter of plot, a means of the author to get his character to move.

Some of the Polish underground scenes are distracting and overly didactic, but the train transport from Warsaw to Auschwitz and the scenes in the commandant's house, which Styron, not trusting to Sophie's English, relates mostly in his own voice, are starkly told, with outrage contained but close to the surface of the prose. The train reaches Cracow at night, "the familiar station, moonlit railroad yard where they lay stranded hour after hour. In the greenish moonglow an extraordinary sight: a German soldier standing in *feldgrau* uniform and with slung rifle, masturbating with steady beat in the half-light of the deserted yard, grinningly exhibiting himself to such curious or indifferent or bemused prisoners as might be looking through the peepholes" (p. 479). A foul act and a grim sight indeed. Or the music in Haus Höss:

> Sophie scarcely ever heard the music, indeed blanked most of it out, for it was never anything but noisy German backyard schmalz, Tyrolean joke songs, yodelers, choirs of glockenspiels and accordions, all infused with recurring strains of treacly *Trauer* and lachrymal outpourings from Berlin cafés and music halls, notably such cries from the heart as "Nur nicht aus Liebe weinen," warbled by Hitler's favorite songbird Zarah Leander and played over and over again with merciless and monotonous obsession by the chatelaine of the manor - Höss's garishly bejeweled and strident wife, Hedwig (p. 230).

Music plays an even more important thematic part in *Sophie's Choice* than it did in *Set This House on Fire*. One remembers *Don Giovanni* booming forth from Cass Kinsolving's apartment; Nathan actually knows the libretto by heart. It is the shared passion for music that cements the bond between Sophie, Nathan and Stingo. Their taste is thoroughly mainline, "music in the grand tradition, nothing remotely popular and very little composed after Franz Schubert, with Brahms being a notable exception" (p. 117). So it is fitting if saddening that at the half-baked funeral service led by the unspeakable Reverend DeWitt, "a whiny Hammond organ" plays Gounod's "Ave Maria" (p. 509). And, most outrageous of all, the welcoming prisoners' band at Auschwitz plays the Argentine tango "La Cumparsita" - "Ba-dum-*ba*-dum!" - while Sophie with her two children faces the S.S. doctor whose task it is to look over the prisoners and send them in two different directions, either straight to the gas at Birkenau or to slave labour at Auschwitz (p. 482)." 'Ich möchte mit dir schlafen'," (p. 481) are his very first words to Sophie, and soon he offers her her choice:

> "You may keep one of your children."
> *"Bitte?"* said Sophie (p. 483).

At this writing *Sophie's Choice* has been on the bestseller list for almost forty weeks, but of course the relation between commercial success and critical acclaim is never predictable. Already in the early sixties, John Aldridge accused Styron of using the clichés of the highbrows to impress the middlebrows, and, at about the same time, Marvin Mudrick clobbered Styron for having "coldly chosen the garden path to the drawing-rooms of the Establishment."[15] Initially *The Confessions of Nat Turner* was a remarkable critical - as well as commercial - success, but soon Herbert Aptheker and the black critics moved to the attack; Richard Gilman, revisiting the novel, assured them they were right on target and sought to teach them how they could have made their case in literary critical terms.[16] During the time of creative exhaustion that followed, Styron worked on a novel about the Marine Corps, but with the continuation of "the filthy war," he abandoned *The Way of the Warrior* and started on *Sophie's Choice*.[17] Meanwhile, with the passage of time, *The Confessions of Nat Turner* regained some of its initial critical esteem.[18] Now with the publication of *Sophie's Choice* Styron's case is wide open again.

University of Nijmegen G.A.M. Janssens

NOTES

1 Norman Mailer, *Advertisements for Myself* (Signet Book 1960 [1959]), p. 415; Styron has answered in kind: "For his own peace of mind I fervently hope that he wins the Nobel Prize" ("The Editor Interviews William Styron," *Modern Occasions* I [Fall 1971], 503); and: "the concept of 'the white Negro' is ... preposterous" ("Overcome," *The New York Review of Books*, 26 September 1963, 18).

2 William Styron, *Sophie's Choice* (New York, 1979), p. 221; all further references are to this edition.

3 William Styron, *The Confessions of Nat Turner* (New York, 1967), p. 4.

4 *Set this House on Fire* "has some of my most passionate and best stuff, and I'm proud to have written it" (Robert K. Morris, "An Interview with William Styron," in *The Achievement of William Styron*, eds. Robert K. Morris and Irving Malin, Athens, Ga., 1975, p. 30). "There was a great amount, an enormous amount, that was cut out of *Set This House on Fire* (James L.W. West III, "A Bibliographer's Interview with William Styron," *Costerus*, N.S., IV, 1975, p. 22).

5 Benjamin DeMott, "Styron's Survivor: An Honest Witness," *Atlantic,* July 1979, 77. Cf. also Robert Alter, "Styron's Stingo," *Saturday Review,* 7 July 1979, 42: "Of Styron's published works, only *Set This House on Fire* for some reason is not alluded to." Elsewhere in *Sophie's Choice,* however, Styron mentions "other works of fiction" (p. 215), which may be taken to include *Set This House on Fire.*

6 Louis D. Rubin, Jr., "Notes on a Southern Writer in Our Time," in *The Achievement of William Styron,* pp. 79-87; Rubin makes the same point more succinctly in "William Styron and Human Bondage," in *The Sounder Few: Essays from the 'Hollins Critic'* (Athens, Ga., 1971), p. 307.

7 William Styron, *Set This House on Fire* (London 1961 [1960]), pp. 39, 152.

8 William Styron, "An Elegy for F. Scott Fitzgerald," *The New York Review of Books,* 28 November 1963, 2.

9 It is surely fortuitous that a Washington hotel clerk who has not quite caught Nathan's name ventures "Mason?" (p. 499).

10 See Andrew Turnbull's biography of *Thomas Wolfe* (New York, 1967) which Styron reviewed for *Harper's Magazine,* April 1968, 96-104.

11 "There was a moment when I think I would have ransomed my soul to meet Wolfe" (Styron's review of Malcolm Cowley, *A Second Flowering, The New York Times Book Review,* 6 May 1973, 8). See also Styron, "The Shade of Thomas Wolfe," *Harper's,* April 1968.

12 Malcolm Cowley, "The Faulkner Pattern," *The New Republic,* 8 October 1951, 19-20.

13 *The New York Review of Books,* 29 June 1978, 10-14.

14 *Sophie's Choice* is dedicated to the memory of Styron's father (1889-1978).

15 Aldridge, "William Styron and the Derivative Imagination," in *Time to Murder and Create: The Contemporary Novel in Crisis* (New York, 1966), p. 49; Mudrick, "Mailer and Styron: Guests of the Establishment," *Hudson Review,* 17 (Autumn 1964), 366.

16 "Nat Turner Revisited," *The New Republic,* 27 April 1968, 23-32.

17 Styron, "In the Jungle," *The New York Review of Books,* 26 September 1968, 11. See James Atlas, "A Talk with William Styron *The New York Times Book Review,* 27 May 1979; Tony Schwartz, "The Choosing of 'Sophie'," *Newsweek,* 28 May 1979; West, "A Bibliographer's Interview;" and expecially Ray Ownbey, "Discussions with William Styron," *Mississippi Quarterly,* 30 (1977), 283-295, and Ben Forkner and Gilbert Schricke, "An Interview with William Styron," *The Southern Review,* X (1974), 923-934.

18 See especially Richard Gray, *The Literature of Memory: Modern Writers of the American South* (London, 1977), pp. 291-305.

"THE MEASURED SELF Vs. THE INSATIABLE SELF:" SOME NOTES ON PHILIP ROTH

"One of my continuing problems as a writer," Philip Roth has said, "has been to find the means to be true to these seemingly inimical realms of experience that I am strongly attached to by temperament and training - the aggressive, the crude, and the obscene, at one extreme, and something a good deal more subtle and, in every sense, refined, at the other."[1] In this essay I propose to discuss the various ways in which Roth handles this problem in three of his novels: *Portnoy's Complaint* (1969), *My Life as a Man* (1974) and *The Professor of Desire* (1977). After a brief discussion of *Portnoy's Complaint,* I shall concentrate my efforts largely on *My Life as a Man* and *The Professor of Desire,* since the obvious similarities between the two novels allow an extensive comparison and reveal in detail how Roth's mastery of his material increases and how he finally succeeds in finding an artistic balance between his "inimical realms of experience."

The inclusion of *Portnoy's Complaint* may seem odd; there is, however, a good deal of continuity in themes and subject matter with the latter novels. In each novel we encounter a highly intelligent, verbally gifted protagonist in his early thirties; all three are academics with a non-intellectual lower middle-class or middle-class Jewish-American background; we find in them the same warring impulses - corresponding to Roth's distinction - and in each case the opposing tendencies within their characters are dramatized through their relationships with women, relationships that often have a self-destructive aspect. Moreover, all three protagonists tell a story, in a confessional mode, of initial and dazzling success, and later apathy and despair. There is, in fact, even a historical continuity between these novels, even though Roth published three books between *Portnoy's Complaint* and *My Life as a Man.* According to Roth, *My Life as a Man* "is a book I'd been writing, abandoning, and returning to ever since I published *Portnoy's Complaint*. Whenever I gave up on it I went to work on one of the 'playful' books - maybe my despair over the difficulties with the one book accounted for why I wanted to be so playful in the others. At any rate, all the while that *My Life as a Man* was simmering away on the 'moral' back burner, I wrote *Our Gang, The Breast,* and *The Great American Novel.*" [2]

I should begin by pointing out that Roth's description of his artistic problem is not precise enough. As I shall demonstrate in the following analyses of his protagonists, the problem is theoretically two-sided, but in practice it has three sides. There are not two possible realms of experience for his protagonists to move in, but there are three: there is the attraction of the obscene, the attraction of the ideal, and the attraction of the sober middle-ground. It seems to me that paradoxically the basic juxtaposition does not exist between the obscene and the ideal, but between these two possibilities on the one hand and sober conventionality on the other. The deepest tension in Alexander Portnoy *(Portnoy's Complaint)*, Peter Tarnopol *(My Life as a Man)* and David Kepesh *(The Professor of Desire)* is the tension between an attachment to that what belongs to ordinary, conventional experience, and a deep desire for adventure, for intensity, for freedom, for the lofty. They are emotionally attached to the middle-ground, its supposed safety and uneventful serenity, yet they also want to venture out into the unknown as far as possible, both in the direction of the obscene and in the direction of the ideal.

In the case of Alexander Portnoy Roth mainly stresses the tension between the middle-ground and the obscene. Admittedly, Portnoy is also supposed to be a committed humanitarian - he is Assistant Commisioner of Human Opportunity - but his desire to improve the world carries no fictional force. His idealism is a token gesture on Roth's part, not to be taken seriously. Portnoy, then, is caught between convention and obscene desires: "torn by desires that are repugnant to my conscience, and a conscience repugnant to my desires."[3] His conventionality is emphasized - rather than dramatized - at various occasions. He is, in some ways, a respectable citizen who does not smoke or use drugs, hardly even drinks, cannot lie, is critical of his father's table manners, and worries a good deal about his reputation. He tells his analyst, Dr Spielvogel, that he does not want a "sexual extravaganza for a life," that he would rather have "simplicity" and "health"(p.184).Envious of those people "who feel in life at ease," who have a "simple and essential affiliation with what is going on"(p.50), he gives Spielvogel a hysterical sketch of his own "idea of a good time": "sitting at home listening to Jack Benny with my kids! Raising intelligent, loving, sturdy children! Protecting some good woman! Dignity! Health! Love! Industry!" (p. 176). It is this side of Portnoy's character that leads him to women like Kay Campbell - "Artless, sweet-tempered, with a trace of morbidity or egoism"(p.153)- and that explains his seemingly hypocritical satisfaction at hearing of the sordid end of a promiscuous girl he knew as an adolescent: "Bad enough, rotten enough, and you get your cock-sucking head blown off by boogies. Now that's the way the world's *supposed* to be run!" (p. 125).

However, there is also Portnoy's tendency towards the crude and the obscene, towards the fascinating extremes of experience. To this side of young Portnoy Kay Campbell comes to seem "boringly predictable in conversation, and about as desirable as blubber in bed" (p.164)and all his later affairs with "lively, intelligent, self-respecting, self-assured, and well-behaved young women" (p.153) end likewise in failure because of the very qualities these girls possess. Much as he is drawn to the conventional virtues, Portnoy is even more repelled by them: "Because to be *bad,* Mother, that is the real struggle: to be bad - and to enjoy it! That is what makes men of us boys, Mother" (p. 87). The conventional life that attracts him is to another side of his character a suffocating trap from which he must escape, and in order to make his escape he must break through the limitations of conventional behaviour. That is why the young Portnoy can regard his "adolescent cock" as his "battering ram to freedom" (p. 23). Roth offers a similar explanation of his protagonist's behaviour. According to him, Portnoy "is obscene because he wants to be saved. An odd, maybe even mad, way to go seeking personal salvation ... Portnoy's pains arise out of his refusal to be bound any longer by taboos which, rightly or wrongly *he* experiences as diminishing and unmanning."[4] Yet, at the same time, Portnoy cannot suppress his own attachment to convention. Every transgression of the conventional code causes intense feelings of guilt or other discomforts. To give one example: after a sexual romp with his current girlfriend and a prostitute they have picked up in the street, poor Portnoy cannot help throwing up. Even when his conscience seems silenced, his body keeps protesting.

Althouth Portnoy's tendency towards the crude and the obscene may not be stronger than his attachment to respectability - after all, each "deviation" causes him "inner hell" - it is his obscenity and his taste for extremes that dominate the novel to the virtual exclusion of the other aspects of his character. Roth allows one of his realms of experience to crowd out the other almost completely - it seems not necessary to offer examples, they abound in the novel - and as a result his novel suffers considerably at the serious level. Portnoy, caught in "the aggressive, the crude, and the obscene," can only present a distorted, caricatural vision of experience and Roth makes no serious attempts to correct his protagonist's vision. Comical as the novel may at times be, it ultimately fails to do justice to its protagonist's problem, not to mention its author's problem. Obviously Roth does not find a balance between his own conflicting impulses.

My Life as a Man is more successful - and therefore more serious - than *Portnoy's Complaint,* since Roth handles his material with a more impartial mind. However, as we shall see, the novel is not a truly balanced achievement.

My Life as a Man consists of two parts, both supposedly written by Peter Tarnopol, a Jewish-American writer in his early thirties. The second part presents Tarnopol's rather chaotic account of his short-lived marriage to Maureen Johnson, whom he has left after a few years of marital anguish, and who has been killed in a car accident about a year before Tarnopol gives us the story of their relationship. The first part of the novel contains two stories, in which Tarnopol fictionally disguises himself as Nathan Zuckerman. The first story "Salad Days," is rather light-hearted and deals mainly with young Zuckerman's enterprising sexual life. The other story, "Courting Disaster," is told soberly and reflectively. Zuckerman is given a different background and the story takes him through a short and desperate marriage up to the point where after the suicide of his wife he is living in exile with his much younger step-daughter. In response to criticisms of this structure, Roth has claimed that Tarnopol's two stories are an integral part of *My Life as a Man:* together with Tarnopol's autobiography they serve to reflect his "struggle to achieve a description."[5] I shall consider the stories, then, as two of Tarnopol's attempts to analyze and understand himself.

Tarnopol's "description" reveals that he, too, has a penchant for conventionality. This is dramatized particularly in his relationship with Susan McCall, the woman he begins an affair with after he has left his wife: "our life together had taken on a predictable and pleasant orderliness - pleasant, for me, for being so predictable. I wanted nothing more than day after day without surprises; just the sort of repetitious experience that drove other people wild with boredom was the most gratifying thing I could manage."[6] But Tarnopol's interest in order and convention is not important in the novel. In fact, *My Life as a Man* mainly emphasizes its protagonist's dissatisfaction with ordinary experience. Over his desk he has a phrase from one of Flaubert's letters:" 'Be regular and orderly in your life like a bourgeois, so that you may be violent and original in your work' " (pp. 174-5). But Tarnopol cannot heed the master's advice:

> for all the discipline and seriousness (and *awe*) with which I approached the Flaubertian vocation, I still wanted my life to be *somewhat* original, and if not violent, at least interesting, when the day's work was done. After all, hadn't Flaubert himself, before he settled down at his round table to become the tormented anchorite of modern literature, gone off as a gentleman-vagabond to the Nile, to climb the pyramids and sow his oats with dusky dancing girls? (p. 175).

Tarnopol's impatience with the ordinariness of life finds expression in the two related impulses outlined earlier in this essay. He wants to transgress the limitations of conventional experience through an intensification and radicalization of experience, simultaneously he wants to lead a life of high idealism. As in *Portnoy's Complaint,* the desire to break through the barriers of convention expresses itself mainly in sexual relationships. The idealist impulse is expressed through Tarnopol's profession as a writer and through his attitude to art and its high moral function.

Tarnopol is obviously aware of these aspects of his character and he uses them as fictional material in his two stories. In "Salad Days" his alter ego, Zuckerman, has a frantic affair with a seventeen-year-old girl, who is his match in sexual inventiveness and daring:"Zuckerman would stare ... at the nude girl writhing, just as he had directed her to, upon the plastic handle of her hairbrush, or her vaginal jelly applicator, or once, upon a zucchini purchased for that purpose earlier in the day" (p. 26). But at the same time

Zuckerman is drawn to "exquisiteness of feeling and refinement of spirit," and to this Zuckerman the girl is "a tantalizing slave and an extraordinary lay, but hardly a soul mate for someone who felt as he did about great writers and great books" (p. 28). "Courting Disaster" further analyzes Zuckerman's idealistic (and rather self-righteous) impulse and shows us how this idealism, together with his desire for intense experience, leads him into his unfortunate marriage.

Tarnopol's own story reveals of course the same pattern. To the young Tarnopol, life as he knows it seems inadequate. He wants more than the experiences life has so far offered him. This urge is already present in his early affair, as a soldier, with a German girl: "I used to be fascinated by whatever she could tell me about her experience of the war" (p. 179). His fascination with the unknown leads Tarnopol directly into the fateful relationship with his later wife. When he meets Maureen, he has an affair with a girl who reminds us of the Ivy League girls Portnoy had ultimately no use for and he ends it abruptly: "In short, because she was rich, pretty, protected, smart, sexy, adoring, young, vibrant, clever, confident, ambitious - that's why I gave her up for Maureen! She was a girl still, who had just about everything. I, I decided at twenty-five, was beyond 'that.' I wanted something called 'a woman' " (p. 178). Compared to Maureen, the girl seems too ordinary. Tarnopol is attracted by Maureen's "terrific energy and spirit" (p. 176), and believes "all [her] reversals and recoveries, all this *movement* of her, to be evidence of a game, audacious, and determined little spirit" (p. 177). As he puts it himself, in retrospect, "Maureen's chaotic, daredevil background had a decidedly exotic and romantic appeal. She had been around - and around. I liked that idea ..." (p. 177). This fascination with what seems to be the real thing, true experience, is fictionalized by Tarnopol himself in "Salad Days," where the young Zuckerman is completely under the spell of his more experienced brother Sherman - "It seemed to the adolescent boy that his older brother had found access to a daring and manly life" (p. 10) - and is fictionalized for Tarnopol by Roth through Tarnopol's choice of books for the great works of fiction course he teaches at Hofstra University: "a course whose core had come to be *The Brothers Karamazov, The Scarlet Letter, The Trial, Death in Venice, Anna Karenina,* and Kleist's *Michael Kohlhaas* derived of course from the professor's steadily expanding extracurricular interest in the subject of transgression and punishment" (p. 233).

Tarnopol is deluded by his own desire for a grander and more daring life and it takes him a good deal of time to find out that Maureen is a pathological liar and lives in illusions of her own making. Then, when he has finally decided to end their relationship once and for all, he becomes the victim of his idealistic streak. Absolutely convinced that the marriage will turn out to be a disaster, he proposes to her when he believes that she is pregnant. Faced with "one of those grim and unyielding predicaments such as [he has] read about in fiction," he takes a "moral," idealistic course: "It seemed then that I was making one of those moral decisions for a young man as morally 'serious' as myself" (p. 194). The fact that he is "so grandiose about [his] honor, [his] integrity, and [his] manly duty, about 'morality' itself" (p. 194), entraps him in a marriage from which it will prove impossible to escape. Emphasizing that character is fate, Roth has Tarnopol behave similarly later in the novel when he meets Susan McCall. At the time, separated from Maureen, Tarnopol is "rather taken" with a "bright and engaging girl," who is passionate to boot, but for seemingly inexplicable reasons he drops the girl for Susan, who is anorgastic and has already "gone completely to pieces on three occasions." Again Tarnopol chooses the woman who seems more experienced and interesting, and in whose life he will be able to play a moral role: he starts a program that aims to educate her academically and sexually and that must give her the self-confidence she lacks. In the meantime, however, Tarnopol has gained insight into himself. Suspicious of his own motives, he cannot bring himself to marry Susan: "I couldn't marry her. I couldn't do it. If and when I was ever to marry again, it would have to be someone in whose wholeness I had an abounding faith and trust" (p. 137). So, at the end of his story, Tarnopol is waiting for the kind of healthy, wholesome woman he has already rejected several times. As long as he remains unable to reconcile his conflicting desires with each other he will remain as paralyzed as he is when the novel ends.

This analysis of Roth's presentation of Tarnopol suggests that he has his problem of the "seemingly inimical realms of experience" better in hand than is actually the case. However, once again "the aggressive, the crude, and the obscene"... are more prominent than the "subtle and ... refined." Roth upsets the balance by saddling Tarnopol with improbable actions and involving him in irrelevant scenes. It is not so much the case that Tarnopol is crude at times, it is rather that Roth is crude *for* him, especially in those scenes that seem left-overs Roth found no use for in *Portnoy's Complaint*. There is, for instance, the passage in which Tarnopol tells Spielvogel - Roth also gives him Portnoy's analyst - of a recent habit he has developed under the stress of his vicious battle with his wife:

> "I didn't hear you. Your sperm? What about your sperm?"
> "My semen - I leave it places."
> "Yes?"
> "I smear it places. I go to people's houses and I leave it - places."
> "You break into people's houses?"
> "No, no," I said sharply - what did he think I was, a madman? "I'm invited. I go to the bathroom. I leave it somewhere ... on the tap. In the soap dish. Just a few drops ..."
> "You masturbate in their bathrooms."
> "Sometimes, yes. And leave ..."
> "Your signature."
> "Tarnopol's silver bullet."

> He smiled at my joke; I did not. I had still more to tell.
> "I've done it at the university library. Smeared it on the bindings of books."
> "Of books? Which books?"
> "Books! Any books! Whatever books are handy!"
> "Anywhere else?"
> I sighed.
> "Speak up, please," said the doctor.
> "I sealed an envelope with it," I said in a loud voice. "My bill to the telephone company" (p. 211).

This is lively stuff, allright, but it is also rather irrelevant. One suspects Roth of using his protagonist for some pyrotechnics. We find the same tendency in the scene where Tarnopol attempts to beat up Maureen. The impulse is entirely credible, but Roth turns the beating into a bizarre and grotesque incident with Maureen spreading her faeces all over Tarnopol's apartment. Tarnopol's excitement over the can opener he finds in Maureen's bedroom is another example of this unnecessary focus on the crude. Convinced that she has used the instrument to masturbate with - " 'Look! Look at this nice sharp metal tooth. How she must love that protruding out of her - how she must love to look down at that!' " (p. 317) - he actually thinks that he will be able to use it in court as evidence of his wife's pervertedness. Or there is the scene in which Tarnopol, on his way home from Maureen's apartment after finding the opener, is thrown out of a cab by an outraged cab driver, because he has held the opener locked between his thighs.

What is worse, however, is that especially "the aggressive" and crude" dominate the presentation of Maureen Tarnopol, thus turning her into an incomprehensible caricature. The aggression that Tarnopol feels (and expresses) towards his estranged wife is credible enough, but Roth seems to share it. This is not only suggested by the way he presents her - consider, for example, her incontinence when Tarnopol attacks her - but also by the way he chooses *not* to present her. In the course of the novel Roth creates a number of opportunities to add depth and complexity to Maureen's character, but he never uses them seriously. There is, for instance, Maureen's diary, which Tarnopol gets to read after her attempt to commit suicide. It reveals virtually nothing that is worth revealing and adds little to what we have already come to know of Maureen through her own words and actions. It seems to me that this is a failure to imagine her on Roth's part. The reader is flooded with Tarnopol's self-analyses (and those offered by Spielvogel), but an analysis of Tarnopol's enemy is not attempted when the fictional situation makes that excellently possible. The same unwillingness to consider Maureen as a real character (and not exclusively through Tarnopol's prejudices) dominates the scene in which Tarnopol meets one of Maureen's former husbands, who has come over after hearing of her suicide attempt. Surprisingly, he is "overjoyed" to hear that she is alive; she is, as he tells Tarnopol, "one of the gamest people" he knows. But this entirely different view of Maureen - from one who has also lived with her - is given short shrift. Roth does not want to present Maureen in any other than crude and caricatural terms. As in *Portnoy's Complaint,* a lack of balance influences and damages his art, even if *My Life as a Man* is by far the better novel.

Three years later, however, Roth appeared to have solved his artistic problem; in *The Professor of Desire* the tension between the two different aspects of the author's personality are kept firmly under control. Indeed, the novel achieves an impressive balance, both in its presentation of the protagonist, David Kepesh, and in its presentation of the other characters, and there is little, if any, material that is not directly functional. The artistic maturity of *The Professor of Desire* is all the more remarkable since there are so many parallels with the earlier novels, in particular with *My Life as a Man*. Just like Tarnopol, Kepesh is a precocious, intelligent child of middle-class Jewish-American parents. He, too, has idealistically devoted himself to literature - as a teacher, not as a creative writer - and tells us the story of his failed marriage and subsequent mental breakdown when he is in his early thirties.

Roth's "seemingly inimical realms of experience" are reflected in two equally important aspects of Kepesh's character and *The Professor of Desire* introduces us directly to this double nature. At nine, the young Kepesh comes under the spell of the twenty-year-old entertainer in his parents' respectable Catskill hotel: "Temptation comes to me first in the conspicuous personage of Herbie Bratasky."[7] He is attracted by "Herbie's shameless exhibitionism" (p. 4) and by his musical and imitative performances, the most daring of which are his perfect simulations of toilet sounds. At the same time, like the good boy he wants to be (and is), he feels guilty over his admiration for Herbie's more dubious accomplishments and dutifully excels at school. A similar dualism characterizes Kepesh's college career. Having developed his own talent for mimicry, he becomes a successful and indefatigable actor in university productions: "There seems to be nothing I cannot do on a stage - there would seem to be nothing that can keep me *off* the stage" (p. 10). But with the next swing of the pendulum he gives up his extraverted behaviour altogether, to turn into "a sober, solitary, rather refined young man devoted to European literature and languages" (p. 12). However, the desire for the extraordinary, for what is beyond the ordinary limits, cannot be repressed. Before long Kepesh comes to despise himself for being "so neat, so clean, so *charming* when the need arises," for being so "pitifully banal" (p. 18) compared to people like his roommate Jelinek, who seems wholly uninterested in the world's opinions and goes his own morose way, reeking of onions. And like Portnoy before him, he begins to seek the extraordinary in pursuit of sex, in "piercing erotic pleasures" (p. 25).

Thus, in the short sketch of Kepesh's early life that opens the novel, Roth clearly sets the pattern that will dominate Kepesh's further experiences as they are told in the rest of the novel. The detailed account of the protagonist's further life begins with his Fulbright year in London, and we find Roth deploying the same strategy we encountered in *Portnoy's Complaint* and *My Life as a Man:* the two sides of Kepesh's character are dramatized through the women he associates with. In London, Kepesh gets involved in a sexual threesome with two Swedish girls, friends of each other. The one girl Birgitta, reflects his lewd tendencies, the other one, Elisabeth, corresponds to his 'good' side.

For Kepesh, too, the desire to transgress conventional norms is connected with a hankering after an elusive freedom. Birgitta "dares to do everything" and she is "sane, clever, courageous, self-possessed - and wildly lascivious!" (p. 49). But what attracts Kepesh most is her "stunning sense of inalienable right with which she does whatever she likes, that total immunity from remorse or self-doubt" (p. 50). She enjoys a freedom that Kepesh envies her and tries to achieve for himself. But he is too much like the other girl, timid, vulnerable Elisabeth, who appears to go along willingly with the sexual experiments Kepesh and Birgitta come up with, but cannot stand the strain and half-heartedly tries to commit suicide. Kepesh is attracted by Birgitta's lasciviousness and freedom, but at the same time he is also drawn towards Elisabeth's innocence and limitations: "Oh, how incredibly moving a thing it is, a person's innocence!" (p. 43). The letter Elisabeth writes him after her return to Sweden spells out how different she is from her compatriot: "I am not a strong girl as Gittan. I am just a weak one Bettan, and I can't do anything about it. It was like being in hell. I was in love with someone and what I did had nothing to do with love. It was like I no more was a human being (p. 33). Kepesh's response to her letter is characteristic: "I am overcome with the most unruly and contradictory emotions - a sense of unworthiness, of loathsomeness, of genuine shame and remorse, and simultaneously as strong a sense that I am not guilty of anything ..." (p. 34). However much Kepesh may want to be like Birgitta, he is too different from her, too 'good.' Initially convinced that he and the girl are "two of a kind" (p. 42), Kepesh realizes that he does not really want her when it dawns on him that she intends to come with him to the United States. Fortunately for him her unsentimentality and toughness save him from an embarrassing situation; she leaves right away, after offering a diagnosis that from her point of view is entirely correct: " 'You are such a boy' " (p. 50).

Character is fate in *The Professor of Desire,* just as in the previous novel, and consequently Kepesh repeats his mistakes. Skipping some years, Roth picks up Kepesh's life again when the latter has almost finished his graduate studies. Kepesh has in the meantime "come to realize that in order to achieve anything lasting," he must "restrain a side of [him]self strongly susceptible to the most bewildering and debilitating sort of temptations, temptations ... inimical to my overall interests" (pp.51-2). But knowledge of one's character does in *My Life as a Man* and *The Professor of Desire* not protect one against its weaknesses. When

Kepesh meets Helen Baird, he becomes the victim of his own fascination with the extraordinary. As he puts it himself, relating his story from the vantage point of tranquil recollection, he "still so need[s] to be intrigued" (p. 65).

Helen seems intriguing indeed. A "nicely brought-up kid from Pasadena," she has run away at eighteen to follow a much older, married business tycoon to Hong Kong, where she became his mistress, leading a life that seems to the initially unbelieving Kepesh too glamorous to be true. But in spite of his doubts, he falls for Helen and her story, attracted by her "fearlessness," by her "determined abandon with which she will give herself to whatever strongly beckons" (p. 62), by her "regal bearing," her "aristocratic sense of herself." (p. 56). Helen is "the enchantress whom [he] had already begun searching for in college" (p. 65), someone who has had the courage to create her own exotic and intense life, regardless of the consequences. To Kepesh she is a "beautiful and dramatic young heroine, who has risked and won and lost so much already, squarely facing up to appetite" (p. 64). Yet, at the same time, Kepesh still has his doubts about his feelings for Helen. Sometimes he cannot help thinking that she has "a banalized conception of self and experience" (p. 57),and at one point, while he is teaching, he catches himself having feelings that belong to a different order of experience, one he cannot see himself sharing with Helen: "all the while I want to ask the chubby girl in the front row, who is rapidly recording my words in her notebook, to become my daughter. I want to look after her and see that she is safe and happy. I want to pay for her clothes and her doctor bills and for her to come and put her arms around me when she is feeling lonely or sad" (p. 74).

But despite these misgivings, Kepesh marries Helen, only to find himself in a hopeless marriage. Tarnopol's misfortune is re-created, but the emphasis is tellingly different. Tarnopol grants that he has been misled by his own romantic conception of women, but he also points an accusing finger at his wife. Kepesh does not put up such a defence. He is his own victim and is willing to admit his delusions, as he is willing to share the blame for the failure of his marriage. Unable to suppress his "strong penchant for orderliness" (p. 153), he finds himself continuously at odds with his magnificently careless and disorderly wife. As he tells his psychiatrist, "'All that nagging at her, at Helen, about the garbage and the laundry and the toast. My mother couldn't have done a better job. About every last detail!'" (pp. 96-7). Living an orderly, well-regulated life as a graduate student, Kepesh is fatally attracted by a woman whose life has been disorderly and undisciplined; married to her, he again insists on order and discipline.

The pattern of Kepesh's character clearly resembles that of Portnoy or of Tarnopol. The warring tendencies, however, are treated more evenly than they were in the earlier novels. And gradually Roth himself begins to make a case for the necessity of balance. Whereas *Portnoy's Complaint* and *My Life as a Man* are largely content to describe, and do not correct their narrator's point of view - in *My Life as a Man* Spielvogel does offer a contrasting view, but it is very difficult to assess its status and its correctness - *The Professor of Desire* offers indirect judgments that either correct Kepesh's views or add perspective to them. This is already true of Roth's presentation of Helen. She is by no means insane, as Maureen is made out to be in *My Life as a Man;* she simply suffers from a more extreme form of Kepesh's own longings for intensity and grandeur. As Kepesh's psychiatrist puts it: " 'What was this search of hers ... but so much evasion, a childish flight from the real attainable projects of a life?' " (p. 99). In support of this diagnosis, Roth undercuts Helen's version of her fabulous relationship with her Hong Kong lover with the information the novel presents. This exposure warns us of course about the illusory character of Kepesh's own desires. His fascination with the daring and the extraordinary is further questioned by Roth's presentation of Ralph Baumgarten, one of Kepesh's colleagues. Like Birgitta, Baumgarten has an "unswerving sense of his own imperatives" (p. 137), and those imperatives concern mainly the gratification of his varied and seemingly inexhaustible sexual desires. Baumgarten's professed disinterestedness in *"menschlichkeit,"* goodness, or virtue, and his uninhibited pursuit of sex, cannot fail to have their appeal for a man like Kepesh: "there are times when, listening to him speak with such shamelessness of the wide range of his satisfactions, I feel that I am in the presence of a parodied projection of myself. A parody - a possibility" (p. 140). But the only time Kepesh lets Baumgarten involve him in one of his sexual expeditions reveals the price that others have to pay for their gratification. Playing the role of two entrepreneurs involved in an erotic picture magazine, they persuade a seventeen-year-old high school girl to come with them to Baumgarten's in a fake "audition." Later, looking at the photographs of his psychiatrist's family in the latter's office, Kepesh realizes that the girl is the former's daughter. He has not only taken advantage of a young girl's naiveté, he has also betrayed the man who patiently and reasonably tries to get him out of his mental impasse. An equally subtle move, on Roth's part, is that the seemingly liberated Baumgarten has not been able to come to terms with his unhappy personal past. As we shall see in a moment, Roth contrasts this with Claire Ovington's - Kepesh's next lover - complete acceptance of an equally unhappy and disorderly past.

Roth's presentation of Claire further emphasizes the necessity of balance. Whereas Helen and Baumgarten are used to illustrate how illusionary and potentially damaging Kepesh's longing for freedom and grandeur is, Claire's life is presented as the alternative to their restless search for intensity and gratification. The child of alcoholic parents whose marriage was one long vicious quarrel, she "has turned all her considerable energy to making normal and ordinary what had for her been heartbreakingly irregular in her childhood home" (p. 160). In contrast to Helen Baird and Kepesh himself, Claire has tried to move towards normalcy and regularity, and with a good deal of success. She has an "innocent and guileless" side that reminds Kepesh of Elisabeth, but she is a good deal stronger. She "never speaks of what she does not have, never lingers for so much as a moment upon loss, misfortune or disappointment" (pp. 220-1); "to every task that presents itself, regardless of how difficult or dreary, she gives her complete attention, taking each up in its turn and steadfastly following it through to its conclusion" (p. 153). As Kepesh tells his psychiatrist, " 'It's awesome, really, the way she deals with each day as it comes, the attention she pays minute by minute. There's no dreaming going on there - just steady, dedicated *living*"' (p. 158).

Claire's strength is emphasized at several points. There is the order she has been able to create in her life after a disorderly youth - in contrast, Baumgarten is shown to be highly undisciplined, not only in his sexual life, but also, for instance, in his rather astonishing table manners. There is her acceptance of her past "as worth recording and remembering" (p. 164), while Baumgarten is unable to use his past for his creative writing, even though he cannot dissociate himself from it. There is the abortion she has without consulting Kepesh - who is not even aware that she is pregnant - because she feels that their relationship is not yet ready for the final step of having a child. Finally, she is able to tell Kepesh that he had better go, no matter the cost to her personally, if he is not prepared for a lasting relationship: " 'But I don't want to give myself any further to something that isn't going to evolve someday into a family. I never had one that made the least bit of sense, and I want one that does' " (p. 224). And, as Kepesh realizes, Claire's tact, poise, confidence and determination are all "marshaled in behalf of something more than high sybaritic adventure" (p. 151). Claire pursues what Kepesh's psychiatrist called "the real attainable projects of a life" (p. 99); her aims are simultaneously more modest and more ambitious than those of Helen, Baumgarten, and Kepesh himself.

Kepesh is strongly drawn towards Claire. Spending the summer with her, in a rented house in the Catskills, he has a sense that he is "living at last in accordance with [his] true spirit" (p. 196). Feeling "home," he is "willing to settle on these terms. This will suffice. No more *more*" (p. 200). He seems to have his desire for more extreme experiences under control, as the dream he had earlier that summer, while vacationing with Claire in Prague, already suggested. In the dream he meets Herbie, his old idol, who takes him to Kafka's whore. Again Herbie represents temptation: " 'We only want to make you happy, to make you finally you, David dear. You have denied yourself too much as it is' " (p. 192). But although Kepesh reluctantly inspects the old woman's vagina, he finally refuses to touch it, even though the offer is free. The scene is comically obscene, but functional: Kepesh is able to resist temptation, even when there seems to be no risk involved. He has also gained more insight into his own predicament through the renewed interest in literature that results from his relationship with Claire. Rereading Chekhov, he sees how the writer "reveals the humiliations and failures - worst of all, the destructive power - of those who seek a way *out* of the shell of restrictions and convention, out of the pervasive boredom and the stifling despair, out of the painful marital situations and the endemic social falsity, into what they take to be a vibrant and desirable life" (p. 156). Perfectly equipped to understand both the desire for such a life and the failures it leads to, he starts a book on "license and restraint in Chekhov's world," aptly dedicated to Claire, whose love has allowed him to find a balance between the two.

But that balance is precarious. Knowing himself, Kepesh is afraid that his contentment cannot last:"'How much longer before I've had a bellyful of wholesome innocence - how long before the lovely blandness of a life with Claire begins to cloy, to pall, and I am out there once again, mourning what I've lost and looking for my way!' " (p. 251). Helen's visit to their idyllic Catskill home seems a bad omen. Remarried to a determined, self-confident, successful man, she is unhappier than ever. Still under the spell of the exotic, the daring, she is too scared to escape from the trap she feels her marriage to be, and seems doomed to suffer for the rest of her life if she does not get a grip on herself. Then, when Kepesh is certain that it is only a matter of time now for him to get tired of Claire - before the orderly, conventionally happy Kepesh "will give way to Herbie's pupil, Birgitta's accomplice, Helen's suiter, yes, to Baumgarten's sidekick and defender" (p. 252) - Roth springs a subtle surprise on the reader.

Almost at the end of the novel, Roth offers a new perspective through a Mr. Barbatnik, a new friend of Kepesh's father, whose life story places Kepesh's troubles in their proper context and at the same time offers an example that Kepesh may profitably follow. A survivor of the Nazi concentration camps, Barbatnik tells at Claire's request the story of his war experiences. Although he has lost his wife and child and all his close relatives, Barbatnik has not become embittered. He is a sober, fair-minded man who has survived the years of hard labour by creating his own illusion: " 'I told myself that this was what I wanted to do. I told myself that this work I was doing was for my child. I told myself different things every single day to make it just that I could last till that night. And that's how I lasted' " (p. 255). And yet he also claims that his major aim in life has been to be " 'A human being ... someone that could see and understand how we lived, and what was real, and not to flatter myself with lies ... To believe in what doesn't exist, no, that wasn't for me' " (p. 257).

Barbatnik's story does not negate Kepesh's troubles, but allows us to judge them from a new perspective. Whereas in *My Life as a Man* Tarnopol's suffering completely dominates his narrative - the references to the social turmoil of the sixties are merely lip-service - *The Professor of Desire* ends with the unequivocal assertion that Kepesh brings his suffering upon himself and that it is not more than personal. Moreover, Barbatnik's strategy for surviving offers an example for Kepesh. He, too, should not believe in what does not exist and not flatter himself with illusions, but use illusions if that is necessary to get a grip on himself, to keep from going to pieces. Paradoxically, illusions may be judiciously used for the sake of soberness.

Of course Kepesh cannot change his character and the message contained in Barbatnik's story cannot easily be put into practice. It is only fitting, then, that Roth decided to leave Kepesh in a state of doubt when the novel ends, still torn between two sides of his character that are both real and permanent. Afraid that "within a year [his] passion will be dead" (p. 261), he can only "pit all [his] accumulated happiness, and all [his] hope against [his] fear of transformations yet to come" (p. 263).

The Professor of Desire presents both of Roth's "seemingly inimical realms of experience" in realistic detail, and achieves thereby a balance that is wholly convincing. As we have seen, it does not only dramatize these opposing forces in its protagonist's behaviour, but shows through the other characters it presents how Kepesh's two conflicting tendencies lead to two kinds of relationships and to two kinds of experience. In *The Professor of Desire* Roth is clearly in control of his material. He keeps both of Kepesh's tendencies firmly in hand, avoiding unnecessary extremes in his presentation of them, and his introduction of Barbatnik serves to give the novel a depth lacking in the earlier ones. If there is no final harmony, in human terms, for David Kepesh - he is at the end of the novel still a professor of literature and there is still the desire - there is for Roth a final harmony in art. He has solved his artistic problem and achieved a balance in art between the crude and the subtle, between the obscene and the refined.

University of Utrecht J.W. Bertens

NOTES

1 Philip Roth, "reading Myself," *Partisan Review,* 40, No. 3 (1973), 409.

2 Philip Roth, *Reading Myself and Others* (London: Jonathan Cape, 1975), p. 112. It is worth pointing out that even in one of the "playful" novels Roth is concerned with his "seemingly inimical realms of experience." *The Breast* deals, according to Roth, partly with "the struggle to accommodate warring (or, at least, contending) impulses and desires, to negotiate some kind of inner peace or balance of power, or perhaps just to maintain hostilities at a low destructive level, between the ethical and

social yearnings and the implacable, singular lusts for the flesh and its pleasures. The measured self vs. the insatiable self."

3 Philip Roth, *Portnoy's Complaint* (New York: Bantam Books 1970), p. 93. Further page references will be given parenthetically after quotation.

4 *Reading Myself and Others,* p. 19.

5 *Reading Myself and Others,* p. 97.

6 Philip Roth, *My Life as a Man* (New York: Holt, Rinehard and Winston, 1974), p. 232. Further page references will be given parenthetically after quotation.

7 Philip Roth, *The Professor of Desire* (New York: Farrar, Straus and Giroux, 1977), p. 3. Further page references will be given parenthetically after quotation.

CURRICULUM VITAE

JACOBUS GERHARDUS RIEWALD was born at Doesburg, a small city on the River IJssel, in the eastern province of Gelderland, on August 15, 1910.

His career, leading from a simple teaching post in a primary school to a full professorship, passing through all the intermediate stages afforded by the Dutch educational system of the time, was typical of what a gifted boy of moderate means, born outside the circles where a university career was normal, might accomplish given time and (above all) perseverance.

Having qualified as a primary school teacher in 1929 (and qualifying as a head teacher two years later) he obtained two certificates in English, followed by further certificates in French and German, and meanwhile, in 1934, qualified for University Entrance.

While still fully employed as an elementary, and later an advanced elementary teacher he then proceeded to read English at the Roman Catholic University at Nijmegen, completing the first degree in 1940 and the second (including full secondary teaching qualifications) in 1946. This got him a post as an English master at Nijmegen. Having meanwhile interested himself in Beerbohm he undertook a critical analysis of the latter's work which, with a brief life and a bibliography, he presented for the degree of Doctor of Philosophy at Nijmegen in 1953 (supervisor Professor T.A. Birrell).

Till the summer of 1960 he continued to serve as an English master at Nijmegen, then, on the invitation of professor R.W. Zandvoort, he moved to Groningen to take up a post as lecturer in English Literature and the didactics of English at the university there.

Meanwhile he had begun to interest himself in American Literature, and in 1951-2 and in 1961, sponsored by the American Government, the Netherlands Foundation for Pure Research (ZWO) and the University of Groningen, he made extended trips to research centres in the USA.

In 1966 his university elected him to a Readership in English & American Literature, converted into a full professorial chair as from January 1980.

Besides originating a steady stream of publications, of which the most important are listed below, he shouldered responsibility in a variety of fields related to that of his principal calling. Thus he served on the boards and in committees of a variety of professional organizations, was instrumental in founding one (part-time) non-university teacher training college and, later, for running a section of a second one (besides teaching in both), and, naturally, sat at one time or another on all the major examining boards.

Two doctoral dissertations were written under his supervision, and a third is expected.
The time has now come for his *otium* — there is no doubt he will not regard it as such.

PUBLICATIONS

A - BOOKS

Sir Max Beerbohm, Man and Writer: A Critical Analysis with a Brief Life and a Bibliography. With a Prefatory Letter by Sir Max Beerbohm. 's-Gravenhage: Martinus Nijhoff, 1953; Brattleboro, Vt.: The Stephen Greene Press, 1961. pp. xxxii, 372 + 4 plates.

A Book of English and American Literature (with L. Grooten and T. Zwartkruis). Hilversum/Antwerpen: Unieboek (Paul Brand).
- I - English Literature to 1900 (1953; 9th ed. 1976) pp. 344, ill.
- II - Twentieth-century English Literature and American Literature (1952; 8th ed. 1976) pp. 376, ill.

The Student's Companion to A Book of English and American Literature (with L. Grooten and T. Zwartkruis). Hilversum/Antwerpen: Unieboek (Paul Brand).
- I - English Literature to 1900 (1955; 7th ed. 1979) pp. 116, ill.
- II - Twentieth-Century English Literature and American Literature (1955; 6th ed. 1970) pp. 144, ill.

Word Study: A Graded English Vocabulary for Dutch Secondary Schools. Bussum: Unieboek (Paul Brand).
- I - The First Thousand Words, Standard Edition (1957; 10th ed. 1976) pp. 190.
- II - The Second Thousand Words (1958; 12th ed. 1978) pp. 142.
- III - The Third Thousand Words (1960; 10th ed. 1978) pp. 158.
- I - The First Thousand Words, Alternative Edition (1971; 2nd ed. 1972) pp. 104.

Moedertaalautomatismen en het Onderwijs in de Levende Talen (with A.J.J. de Witte, S.G.W. van der Meer, en J.P. van der Linden). 's-Hertogenbosch: Malmberg, 1960. pp. 164.

Max in Verse: Parodies and Rhymes by Max Beerbohm (critical text edition). With a Foreword by S.N. Behrman. London: William Heinemann, 1963 / Brattleboro, Vt.: The Stephen Greene Press, 1964. pp. 170. Paperback reissue, The Stephen Greene Press, 1970.

Autogene Symbolen in de poëzie van Robert Lowell. Openbare les gegeven bij de aanvaarding van het ambt van lektor in de Engelse en

Amerikaanse letterkunde aan de Rijksuniversiteit te Groningen. Groningen: Wolters, 1967. pp. 24.

Studie-oriëntatie en Studietechniek. Lezing gehouden ter gelegenheid van de opening van het 22ste studiejaar van de Noordelijke Leergangen onder auspiciën van de Fryske Akademy. Leeuwarden: Fryske Akademy, 1968. pp. 36.

Reynier Jansen of Philadelphia, Early American Printer: A Chapter in Seventeenth-Century Nonconformity. Groningen: Wolters-Noordhoff, 1970. pp. xiv, 296 + 15 plates. (Groningen Studies in English, 11.)

Nieuw Engels Woordenboek: De meest voorkomende Engelse woorden en uitdrukkingen in zinsverband, met hun Nederlandse ekwivalent. Bussum: Unieboek (Paul Brand), 1974. pp. 384.

The Surprise of Excellence: Modern Essays on Max Beerbohm. Hamden, Ct.: Archon Books, 1974. pp. xiv, 266; front.

Perspectives in British and American Literature: A Survey for Students (with L. Grooten). Bussum: Unieboek (Paul Brand), 1974. pp. xii, 200 + 12 plates.

Engels Idioomwoordenboek: De meest voorkomende Engelse woorden en uitdrukkingen in zinsverband, met hun Nederlandse ekwivalent. Bussum: Unieboek (Paul Brand), 1977. pp. 384. Revised edition of *Nieuw Engels Woordenboek* (1974).

Beerbohm's Literary Caricatures: From Homer to Huxley. Hamden, Ct.: Archon Books; London: Penguin Books, Allen Lane, 1977. pp. 296 + 105 ill.

The Critical Reception of American Literature in the Netherlands, 1824-1900: A Documentary Conspectus from Contemporary Periodicals (with J. Bakker). (to be published.)

B - ARTICLES

1 - English and American Literature

"Sir Thomas Browne's Supposed Visit to the Continent," *English Studies*, 28 (1947) 171-3.

"Sir Max Beerbohm," *Handelingen van het Twintigste Nederlands Philologencongres*, Groningen: Wolters, 1948, pp. 77-9.

Some 1300 (original and rewritten) articles as general editor for English and American Literature for the second edition of *De Katholieke Encyclopaedie*, Amsterdam/Antwerpen, 1949-55, 25 vols.

Letter to the Editor, *Times Literary Supplement,* 26 February 1954, 137.

25 articles "Wij vestigen de aandacht op ... Voor Engels" (current bibliography of new English and American books in the field of English and American Language and Literature), *Levende Talen,* October 1955 - October 1960.

"Laureates in Elysium: Sir William Davenant and Robert Southey," *English Studies,* 37 (1956) 133-40 (Visser Anniversary Number).

Contributions to the Current Bibliography of the *Keats-Shelley Journal* (New York), 7-17 (1958-67) *passim.*

"Some Later Elizabethan and Early Stuart Actors and Mucicians," *English Studies,* 40 (1959) 33-41.

"New Light on the English Actors and Musicians in the Netherlands, c. 1590 - c. 1660," *English Studies,* 41 (1960) 65-92.

"De Geschiedenis van de Quakers in Friesland." Voordracht gehouden voor de Noordelijke Tak van de Maatschappij der Nederlandse Letterkunde op 23 maart 1963, *It Beaken: Tydskrift fan de Fryske Akademy,* 25 (September 1963) 185-208; plate.

"Unpublished Parodies," *The Atlantic Monthly,* 212:2 (August 1963) 76-7.

"Shakespeare Burlesque in John Webster's *The Duchess of Malfi,*" *English Studies Presented to R.W. Zandvoort on the Occasion of his Seventieth Birthday,* Amsterdam: Swets & Seitlinger, 1964, pp. 177-89.

"Parody as Criticism," *Neophilologus,* 50 (1966) 125-48; and compare *Handelingen van het Achtentwintigste Nederlands Filologencongres,* Groningen: Wolters, 1964, pp. 139-41.

"Sir Max Beerbohm," *Encyclopedia of World Literature in the Twentieth Century,* vol. 1, New York: Frederick Ungar, 1967.

Letter to the Editor, *Times Literary Supplement,* 19 September 1975, 1063.

"From Naturalism to Lyrical Realism: Fourteen Unpublished Letters from George Moore to Frans Netscher," *English Studies,* 58 (1977) 118-50.

"The Translational Reception of American Literature in Europe, 1800-1900: A Review of Research," *English Studies,* 60 (1979) 562-92.

2 - The Teaching of English as a Foreign Language

"De wetenschappelijke basis van het onderwijs in het Engels" (with G. Storms), *Levende Talen,* April 1954, 155-77.

"Naar aanleiding van vier belangrijke artikelen over het aanvangsonderwijs in de levende vreemde talen," *Levende Talen,* June 1955, 296-306.

"Vragenlijst Levende Talen" (with C. Brouwer and D.M. van Willigen), *Levende Talen,* June 1955, 322-27.

"Moedertaal- en vreemde talenonderwijs" (with A.J.J. de Witte), *Levende Talen,* April 1956, 177-87.

"Leerstof en Methode van het Vreemde-talenonderwijs," *Paedagogische Studiën,* 39 (1956) 178-87.

"Degree of Mastery of the Sound System of a Foreign Language," *VIe Congrès de la Fédération Internationale des Professeurs de Langues Vivantes,* Groningen, 1956, pp. 82-4.

Contributions to a number of articles published by the Didactics Committee of the "Vereniging van Leraren in Levende Talen"(Society of Teachers of Living Languages), *Levende Talen,* 1957-60, *passim.*

"Vocabularium voor het Vreemde-talenonderwijs in het eerste leerjaar," *Levende Talen,* February, April, 1958, 127-43, 235-58 (with others).

"Gemakkelijk herkenbare woorden voor het eerste jaar Engels," *Levende Talen,* April 1959, 222-28 (with others).

"Idioomlijst voor het Onderwijs in het Eerste Leerjaar Engels," *Levende Talen,* December 1960, 621-31.

C - DOCTORAL DISSERTATIONS SUPERVISED

Rudolf BREMER, *Gerard Manley Hopkins: The Sonnets of 1865.* Groningen, 1978. pp. xvi, 208.

Leo Martin van NOPPEN, *Gerard Manley Hopkins, "The Wreck of the Deutschland."* Groningen, 1980. pp. xii, 243.

To this list should be added a considerable number of shorter notes in all fields, as well as some seventy book reviews in *DQR, English Studies, Levende Talen, Neophilologus,* and other journals.

TABULA GRATULATORUM

Professor F.G.A.M. Aarts

Professor W.J. Aerts

Professor and Mrs J.C. Arens

Dr Mary-Jo Arn

J.T.J. Bak

Dr and Mrs J. Bakker

J.L. Baning

Dr and Mrs W.J.A.M. Beek

Mr and Mrs F.Th. Bergefurt

Mr and Mrs A.H.G.F. Bergmans

Dr J.W. Bertens

Professor S. Betsky-Zweig

Professor T.A. Birrell

Mr and Mrs J.M. Blom

J. Boswinkel

Dr and Mrs M.H. Braaksma

J.L. Broekhuis-Nehls

G.H.V. Bunt

Dr P.P.J. van Caspel

J.C. Doodkorte

Professor J.A. van Ek

Professor L.J. Engels

Professor J. Ensink

P. Floor

Professor A.J. Fry

Mr and Mrs P.H.M. van Genugten

Professor and Mrs J. Gerritsen

H. Gort

Louis and Christine Grooten-Mertens

Marie-Louise Grooten

T.L. D'Haen

Ken Heinrich

Professor A.G.F. van Holk

Professor G.A.M Janssens

Mr and Mrs J.A. de Jong

M.J.C. Kloosterhuis-Loggers

Dr A.M.L. Knuth

P.J.A. van Lier

A.H. MacKinnon

Professor Amy van Marken

G. van der Meer

Professor H.H. Meier

J.C. van Meurs

Professor J.J.A. Mooij

Mr and Mrs W.H.J. Mutsaers

Dr Charles R. Nash

Professor W. Noomen

L.M. van Noppen

Professor H.T. Oostendorp

Professor N.E. Osselton

M.B. Portheine

J. Posthumus

Mr and Mrs H.R.J. Riewald

J.R.H. Riewald

N.J. Robat

Professor and Mrs Richard Ruland

Professor W. Schönau

Dr N.H.G. Schoonderwoerd

F.G.F. Schulte

Dr H.I. Schvey

Mrs H.H.M. Sluyters-Janssen

M. Stam

Stichting Noordelijke Leergangen

Professor and Mrs G. Storms

Professor J.A. Tans

J.B.M. Tilman

John Tobias

Dr R.K. Todd

Dr J.A. Verleun

P.M. Vermeer

E.A.M.I. Verpalen

P.J. de Voogd

Professor A.L. Vos

Dr H.J. de Vriend

J. de Vries

E.J. Waltheer

A.C. Wedema

Dr H. Chr. Wekker

Mr and Mrs E.P.J. Wentink

T.A. Westendorp

Professor and Mrs D.R.M. Wilkinson

C.J.J. de Witt Wijnen

Professor R.W. Zandvoort

Mr and Mrs D. van der Zee

T.H.J. Zwartkruis, Bishop of Haarlem

ADDENDA

Professor Seymour Betsky

Mrs Stephen Greene

Rodopi

COSTERUS. Essays in English and American Language and Literature.

Volume 1. Amsterdam 1972. 240 p. Hfl. 40.–
GARLAND CANNON: Sir William Jones's Translation-Interpretation of Sanskrit Literature. SARAH DYCK: The Presence of that Shape: Shelley's *Prometheus Unbound.* MARJORIE ELDER: Hawthorne's *The Marble Faun:* A Gothic Structure. JAMES L. GOLDEN: Adam Smith as a Rhetorical Theorist and Literary Critic. JACK GOODSTEIN: Poetry, Religion and Fact: Matthew Arnold. JAY L. HALIO: Anxiety in *Othello.* JOHN ILLO: Miracle in Milton's Early Verse. F. SAMUEL JANZOW: De Quincey's "Danish Origin of the Lake Country Dialect" Republished. MARTIN L. KORNBLUTH: The Degeneration of Classical Friendship in Elizabethan Drama. VIRGINIA MOSELY: The "Dangerous" Paradox in Joyce's "Eveline". JOHN NIST: Linguistics and the Esthetics of English. SCOTT B. RICE: Smollett's *Travels* and the Genre of Grand Tour Literature. LISBETH J. SACHS and BERNARD H. STERN: The Little Preoedipal Boy in Papa Hemingway and How He Created His Artistry.

Volume 2. Amsterdam 1972. 236 p. Hfl. 40.–
RALPH BEHRENS: Mérimée, Hemingway, and the Bulls. JEANNINE BOHLMEYER: Mythology in Sackville's "Induction" and "Complaint". HAROLD A. BRACK: Needed – a new language for communicating religion. LEONARD FEINBERG: Satire and Humor: In the Orient and in the West. B. GRANGER: The Whim-Whamsical Bachelors in Salmagundi. W. M. FORCE: The What Story? or Who's Who at the Zoo? W. N. KNIGHT: To Enter lists with God. Transformation of Spencerian Chivalric Tradition in Paradise Regained. MARY D. KRAMER: The Roman Catholic Cleric on the Jacobean Stage. BURTON R. POLLIN: The Temperance Movement and Its Friends Look at Poe. SAMUEL J. ROGAL: Two Translations of the Iliad, Book I: Pope and Tickell. J. L. STYAN: The Delicate Balance: Audience Ambivalence in the Comedy of Shakespeare and Chekhov. CLAUDE W. SUMERLIN: Christopher Smart's A Song to David: its influence on Robert Browning. B.W. TEDFORD: A Recipe for Satire and Civilization. H. H. WATTS: Othello and the Issue of Multiplicity. GUY R. WOODALL: Nationalism in the Philadelphia National Gazette and Literary Register: 1820–1836.

Volume 3. Amsterdam 1972. 236 p. Hfl. 40.–
RAYMOND BENOIT: In Dear Detail by Ideal Light: "Ode on a Grecian Urn". E. F. CALLAHAN: Lyric Origins of the Unity of 1 Henry IV. FRASER DREW: John Masefield and Juan Manuel de Rosas. LAURENCE GONZALEZ: Persona Bob: seer and fool. A. HIRT: A Question of Excess: Neo-Classical Adaptations of Greek Tragedy. EDWIN HONIG: Examples of

Poetic Diction in Ben Jonson. ELSIE LEACH: T. S. Eliot and the School of Donne. SEYMOUR REITER: The Structure of 'Waiting for Godot'. DANIEL E. VAN TASSEL: The Search for Manhood in D. H. Lawrence's 'Sons and Lovers'. MARVIN ROSENBERG: Poetry of the Theatre. GUY R. WOODALL: James Russell Lowell's "Works of Jeremy Taylor, D.D.'

Volume 4. Amsterdam 1972. 233 p. Hfl. 40.–
BOGDDY ARIAS: Sailor's Reveries. R. H. BOWERS: Marlowe's 'Dr. Faustus', Tirso's 'El Condenado por Desconfiado', and the Secret Cause. HOWARD O. BROGAN: Satirist Burns and Lord Byron. WELLER EMBLER: Simone Weil and T. S. Eliot. E. ANTHONY JAMES: Defoe's Autobiographical Apologia: Rhetorical Slanting in 'An Appeal to Honour and Justice'. MARY D. KRAMER: The American Wild West Show and "Buffalo Bill" Cody. IRVING MASSEY: Shelley's "Dirge for the Year": The Relation of the Holograph to the First Edition. L. J. MORRISSEY: English Street Theatre: 1655–1708. M. PATRICK: Browning's Dramatic Techniques and 'The Ring and the Book': A Study in Mechanic and Organic Unity. VINCENT F. PETRONELLA: Shakespeare's 'Henry V' and the Second Tetralogy: Meditation as Drama. NASEEB SHAHEEN: Deriving Adjectives from Nouns. TED R. SPIVEY: The Apocalyptic Symbolism of W. B. Yeats and T. S. Eliot. EDWARD STONE: The Other Sermon in 'Moby–Dick'. M. G. WILLIAMS: 'In Memoriam': A Broad Church Poem.

Volume 5. Amsterdam 1972. 236 p. Hfl. 40.–
PETER G. BEIDLER: Chaucer's Merchant and the Tale of January. ROBERT A. BRYAN: Poets, Poetry, and Mercury in Spenser's Prosopopia: Mother Hubberd's Tale. EDWARD M. HOLMES: Requiem For A Scarlet Nun. E. ANTHONY JAMES: Defoe's Narrative Artistry: Naming and Describing in Robinson Crusoe. MICHAEL J. KELLY: Coleridge's "Picture, or The Lover's Resolution": its Relationship to "Dejection" and its Sources in the Notebooks. EDWARD MARGOLIES: The Playwright and his Critics. MURRAY F. MARKLAND: The Task Set by Valor. RAYMOND S. NELSON: Back to Methuselah: Shaw's Modern Bible. THOMAS W. ROSS: Maimed Rites in Much Ado About Nothing. WILLIAM B. TOOLE: The Metaphor of Alchemy in Julius Caesar, PAUL WEST: Carlyle's Bravura Prophetics. GLENA D. WOOD: The Tragi-Comic Dimensions of Lear's Fool. H. ALAN WYCHERLEY: "Americana": The Mencken – Lorimer Feud.

Volume 6. Amsterdam 1972. 235 p. Hfl. 40.–
GEORG W. BOSWELL: Superstition and Belief in Faulkner. ALBERT COOK: Blake's Milton. MARSHA KINDER: The Improved Author's Farce: An Analysis of the 1734 Revisions. ABE LAUFE: What Makes Drama Run? (Introduction to Anatomy of a Hit). RICHARD L. LOUGHLIN: Laugh and Grow Wise with Oliver Goldsmith. EDWARD MARGOLIES: The American Detective Thriller & The Idea of Society. RAYMOND S. NELSON: Shaw's Heaven, Hell, and Redemption. HAROLD OREL: Is Patrick White's Voss the Real Leichhardt of Australia? LOUIS B. SALOMON: A Walk With Emerson On The Dark Side. H. GRANT SAMPSON: Structure in the Poetry of Thoreau. JAMES H. SIMS, Some Biblical Light on Shakespeare's Hamlet.

ROBERT F. WILLSON, Jr.: Lear's Auction. JAMES N. WISE: Emerson's "Experience" and "Sons and Lovers". JAMES D. YOUNG: Aims in Reader's Theatre.

Volume 7. Amsterdam 1973. 235 p. Hfl. 40.–
HANEY H. BELL Jr.: Sam Fathers and Ike McCaslin and the World in Which Ike Matures. SAMUEL IRVING BELLMAN: The Apocalypse in Literature. HALDEEN BRADDY: England and English before Alfred. DAVID R. CLARK: Robert Frost: "The Thatch" and "Directive". RALPH MAUD: Robert Crowley, Puritan Satirist. KATHARINE M. MORSBERGER: Hawthorne's "Borderland": The Locale of the Romance. ROBERT E. MORSBERGER: The Conspiracy of the Third International. "What is the metre of the dictionary?" – Dylan Thomas. RAYMOND PRESTON: Dr. Johnson and Aristotle. JOHN J. SEYDOW: The Sound of Passing Music: John Neal's Battle for American Literary Independence. JAMES H. SIMS: Enter Satan as Esau, Alone; Exit Satan as Belshazzar: *Paradise Lost,* BOOK (IV). MICHAEL WEST, Dryden and the Disintegration of Renaissance Heroic Ideals. RENATE C. WOLFF: Pamela as Myth and Dream.

Volume 8. Amsterdam 1973. 231 p. Hfl. 40.–
SAMUEL I. BELLMAN: Sleep, Pride, and Fantasy: Birth Traumas and Socio-Biologic Adaptation in the American-Jewish Novel. PETER BUITENHUIS: A Corresponding Fabric: The Urban World of Saul Bellow. DAVID R. CLARK: An Excursus upon the Criticism of Robert Frost's "Directive". FRANCIS GILLEN: Tennyson and the Human Norm: A Study of Hubris and Human Commitment in Three Poems by Tennyson. ROBERT R. HARSON: H. G. Wells: The Mordet Island Episode. JULIE B. KLEIN: The Art of Apology: "An Epistle to Dr. Arbuthnot" and "Verses on the Death of Dr. Swift". ROBERT E. MORSBERGER: The Movie Game in Who's Afraid of Virginia Woolf and The Boys in the Band. EDWIN MOSES: A Reading of "The Ancient Mariner". JOHN H. RANDALL: Romeo and Juliet in the New World. A Study in James, Wharton, and Fitzgerald "Fay ce que vouldras". JOHN E. SAVESON: Conrad as Moralist in Victory. ROBERT M. STROZIER: Politics, Stoicism, and the Development of Elizabethan Tragedy. LEWIS TURCO: Manoah Bodman: Poet of the Second Awakening.

Volume 9. Amsterdam 1973. 251 p. Hfl. 40.–
THOMAS E. BARDEN: Dryden's Aims in *Amphytryon.* SAMUEL IRVING BELLMAN: Marjorie Kinnan Rawling's Existentialist Nightmare *The Yearling.* SAMUEL IRVING BELLMAN: Writing Literature for Young People. Marjorie Kinnan Rawlings' "Secret River" of the Imagination. F. S. JANZOW: "Philadelphus," A New Essay by De Quincey. JACQUELINE KRUMP: Robert Browning's Palace of Art. ROBERT E. MORSBERGER: The Winning of Barbara Undershaft: Conversion by the Cannon Factory, or "Wot prawce selvytion nah?" DOUGLAS L. PETERSON: Tempest-Tossed Barks and Their Helmsmen in Several of Shakespeare's Plays. STANLEY POSS: Serial Form and Malamud's Schlemihls. SHERYL P. RUTLEDGE: Chaucer's Zodiac of Tales. CONSTANCE RUYS: John Pickering–Merchant Adventurer and Playwright. JAMES H. SIMS: Death in Poe's Poetry: Varia-

tions on a Theme. ROBERT A. SMITH: A Pioneer Black Writer and the Problems of Discrimination and Miscegenation. ALBERT J. SOLOMON: The Sound of Music in "Eveline": A Long Note on a Barrel-Organ. J. L. STYAN: Goldsmith's Comic Skills. ARLINE R. THORN: Shelley's *The Cenci* as Tragedy. E. THORN: James Joyce: Early Imitations of Structural Unity. LEWIS TURCO: The Poetry of Lewis Turco. An Interview by Gregory Fitzgerald and William Heyen.

New Series. Volume 1. Edited by James L. W. West III. Amsterdam 1974. 194 p. Hfl. 40.–
D. W. ROBERTSON, Jr.: Chaucer's Franklin and His Tale. CLARENCE H. MILLER and CARYL K. BERREY: The Structure of Integrity: The Cardinal Virtues in Donne's "Satyre III". F. SAMUEL JANZOW: The English Opium-Eater as Editor. VICTOR A. KRAMER: Premonition of Disaster: An Unpublished Section for Agee's *A Death in the Family*. GEORGE L. GECKLE: Poetic Justice and *Measure for Measure*. RODGER L. TARR: Thomas Carlyle's Growing Radicalism: The Social Context of *The French Revolution*. G. THOMAS TANSELLE: Philip Gaskell's *A New Introduction to Bibliography*. Review Essay. KATHERINE B. TROWER: Elizabeth D. Kirk's *The Dream Thought of Piers Plowman*. Review Essay. JAMES L. WEST III: Matthew J. Bruccoli's *F. Scott Fitzgerald a Descriptive Bibliography*. Review Essay. JAMES E. KIBLER: R. W. Stallman's *Stephen Crane: A Critical Bibliography*. Review. ROBERT P. MILLER: Jonathan Saville's *The Medieval Erotic Alba*. Review.

New Series. Volume 2. **THACKERY. Edited by Peter L. Shillingsburg.** Amsterdam 1974. 359 p. Hfl. 70.–
JOAN STEVENS: *Vanity Fair* and the London Skyline. JANE MILLGATE: History *versus* Fiction: Thackeray's Response to Macaulay. ANTHEA TRODD: Michael Angelo Titmarsh and the Knebworth Apollo. PATRICIA R. SWEENEY: Thackeray's Best Illustrator. JOAN STEVENS: Thackeray's Pictorial Capitals. ANTHONY BURTON: Thackeray's Collaborations with Cruikshank, Doyle, and Walker. JOHN SUTHERLAND: A *Vanity Fair* Mystery: The Delay in Publication. JOHN SUTHERLAND: Thackeray's Notebook for *Henry Esmond*. EDGAR F. HARDEN: The Growth of *The Virginians* as a Serial Novel: Parts 1–9. GERALD C. SORENSEN: Thackeray Texts and Bibliographical Scholarship. PETER L. SHILLINSBURG: Thackeray Texts: A Guide to Inexpensive Editions. RUTH apROBERTS: Thackeray Boom: A Review. JOSEPH E. BAKER: Reading Masterpieces in Isolation: Review. ROBERT A. COLBY and JOHN SUTHERLAND: Thackeray's Manuscripts: A Preliminary Census of Library Locations.

New Series. Volume 3. Edited by James L. W. West III. Amsterdam 1975. 184 p. Hfl. 40.–
SAMUEL J. ROGAL: Hurd's Editorial Criticism of Addison's Grammar and Usage. ROBERT P. MILLER: Constancy Humanized: Trivet's Constance and the Man of Law's Custance. WELDON THORNTON: Structure and Theme in Faulkner's *Go Down, Moses*. JAYNE K. KRIBBS: John Davis: A Man For His Time. STEPHEN E. MEATS: The Responsibilities of an Editor of Correspon-

dence. Review Essay. RODGER L. TARR: Carlyle and Dickens *or* Dickens and Carlyle. Review. CHAUNCEY WOOD: Courtly Lovers: An Unsentimental View. Review.

New Series. Volume 4. Edited by James L. W. West III. Amsterdam 1975. 179 p. Hfl. 40.–
JAMES L. W. WEST III: A Bibliographer's Interview with William Styron. J. TIMOTHY HOBBS: The Doctrine of Fair Use in the Law of Copyright. JUNE STEFFENSEN HAGEN: Tennyson's Revisions of the Last Stanza of "Audley Court". CLIFFORD CHALMERS HUFFMAN: *The Christmas Prince*: University and Popular Drama in the Age of Shakespeare. ROBERT L. OAKMAN: Textual Editing and the Computer. Review Essay. T.H. HOWARD-HILL: The Bard in Chains: *The Harvard Concordance to Shakespeare.* Review Essay. BRUCE HARKNESS: Conrad Computerized and Concordanced. Review Essay. MIRIAM J. SHILLINGSBURG: A Rose is a Four-Letter Word; or, The Machine Makes Another Concordance. Review Essay. RICHARD H. DAMMERS: Explicit Statement as Art. Review Essay. A. S. G. EDWARDS: Medieval Madness and Medieval Literature. Review Essay. NOEL POLK: Blotner's Faulkner. Review.

New Series. Volume 5–6. **GYASCUTUS. Studies in Antebellum Southern Humorous and Sporting Writing. Edited by James L. W. West III.** Amsterdam 1978.
NOEL POLK: The Blind Bull, Human Nature: Sut Lovingood and the Damned Human Race. HERBERT P. SHIPPEY: William Tappan Thompson as Playwright. LELAND H. COX, Jr.: Porter's Edition of *Instructions to Young Sportsmen.* ALAN GRIBBEN: Mark Twain Reads Longstreet's *Georgia Scenes.* T. B. THORPE's Far West Letters, ed. Leland H. Cox, Jr. An Unknown Tale by GEORGE WASHINGTON HARRIS ed. William Starr. JOHNSON JONES HOOPER's "The 'Frinnolygist' at Fault" ed. James L. W. West III. SOUTH CAROLINA WRITERS in the *Spirit of the Times* ed. Stephen E. Meats. A NEW MOCK SERMON ed. James L. W. West III. ANOTHER NEW MOCK SERMON ed. A. S. Wendel. The PORTER-HOOPER Correspondence ed. Edgar E. Thompson.

New Series. Volume 7. **SANFORD PINSKER: The Languages of Joseph Conrad.** Amsterdam 1978. 87 p. Hfl. 20.–
Table of Contents: Foreword. Introductory Language. The Language of the East. The Language of Narration. The Language of the Sea. The Language of Politics. *Victory* As Afterword.

New Series. Volume 8. **GARLAND CANNON: An Integrated Transformational Grammar of the English Language.** Amsterdam 1978. 315 p. Hfl. 60.–
Table of Contents: Preface. 1) A Child's Acquisition of His First Language. 2) Man's Use of Language. 3) Syntactic Component: Base Rules. 4) Syntactic Component: Lexicon. 5) Syntactic Component: Transformational Rules. 6) Semantic Component. 7) Phonological Component. 8) Man's Understanding of His Language. Appendix: the Sentence-Making Model. Bibliography. Index.

New Series: Volume 9. **GERALD LEVIN: Richardson the Novelist: The Psychological Patterns.** Amsterdam 1978. 172 p. Hfl. 30.–
Table of Contents: Preface. Chapter One. The Problem of Criticism. Chapter Two. "Conflicting Trends" in *Pamela.* Chapter Three. Lovelace's Dream. Chapter Four. The "Family Romance" of *Sir Charles Grandison.* Chapter Five. Richardson's Art. Chapter Six. Richardson and Lawrence: the Rhetoric of Concealment. Appendix. Freud's Theory of Masochism. Bibliography.

New Series: Volume 10. **WILLIAM F. HUTMACHER: Wynkyn de Worde and Chaucer's Canterbury Tales. A Transcription and Collation of the 1498 Edition with Caxton^2 from the General Prologue Through the Knights Tale.** Amsterdam 1978. 224 p. Hfl. 40,–
Table of Contents: Introduction. Wynkyn's Life and Works. Wynkyn De Word's Contribution to Printing. Significance of Wynkyn's *The Canterbury Tales*. Significance of Wynkyn's Order of the Tales. Scheme of the Order of *The Canterbury Tales*. Wynkyn's Variants from CX^2. Printer's Errors. Spelling. Omissions in Wynkyn's Edition. Additions in Wynkyn's Edition. Transpositions in Wynkyn's Edition. Miscellaneous Variants in the Reading. Bibliography. Explanation of the Scheme of the Transcription and Recording of the Variants. The Transcription and Collation.

New Series: Volume 11. **WILLIAM R. KLINK: S. N. Behrman: The Major Plays.** Amsterdam 1978. 272 p. Hfl. 45,–
Table of Contents: Introduction. *The Second Man. Brief Moment. Biography. Rain From Heaven. End of Summer. No Time for Comedy. The Talley Method. But For Whom Charlie.* Language. Conclusion. Bibliography.

New Series: Volume 12. **VALERIE BONITA GRAY: *Invisible Man's* Literary heritage: *Benito Cereno* and *Moby Dick*.** Amsterdam 1978. 145p. Hfl. 30,–
Table of Contents: Democracy: The Politics of "Affirming the Principle" and Celebrating the Individual. The Spectrum of Ambiguity: From Mask Wearing to Shape-shifting. Whiteness or Blackness: Which Casts the Shadow? Melville's and Ellison's Methodology: Bird Imagery and Whale and Circus Lore. Social Protest. Bibliography.

New Series: Volume 13. **VINCENT DIMARCO and LESLIE PERELMAN: The Middle English Letter of Alexander to Aristotle.** Amsterdam 1978. 194p. Hfl. 40,–

New Series: Volume 14. **JOHN W. CRAWFORD: Discourse: Essays on English and American Literature.** Amsterdam 1978. 200p. 40,–
Contents: Chaucer's Use of Sun Imagery. The Fire from Spenser's Dragon: "The Faerie Queene," I.xi. The Changing Renaissance World in Thomas Deloney's Fiction. Shakespeare's Falstaff: A Thrust at Platonism. The Religious Question in *Julius Caesar.* Teaching *Julius Caesar:* A Study in Poetic Persuasion. Shakespeare: A Lesson in Communications. Intuitive Knowledge in *Cymbeline*. White Witchcraft in Tudor-Stuart Drama. Another

Biblical Allusion in *Paradise Lost. Absalom and Achitophel;* and Milton's *Paradise Lost.* Asem-Goldsmith's Solution to Timon's Dilemma. Dr. Johnson: A Modern Example of Christian Constancy. A Unifying Element in Tennyson's *Maud.* Arnold's Relevancy to the Twentieth Century. Sophocles' Role in "Dover Beach". Lest We Forget, Lest We Forget: Kipling's Warning to Humanity. The Garden Imagery in *Great Expectations.* "Victorian" Women in *Barchester Towers.* Another Look at "Youth". Forster's "The Road from Colonus". Biblical Influences in *Cry, the Beloved Country.* Huxley's *Island:* A Contemporary *Utopia.* The Generation Gap in Literature. Bred and Bawn in a Briar Patch – Deception in the Making. Success and Failure in the Poetry of Edwin Arlington Robinson. Naturalistic Tendencies in *Spoon River Anthology.* Primitiveness in "The Bravest Boat". Theme of Suffering in "Sonny's Blues". Nabokov's "First Love". The Temper of Romanticism in *Travels with Charley.* Unrecognized Artists in American Literature: Chicano Renaissance.

New Series: Volume 15. **ROBERT F. WILLSON, JR.: Landmarks of Shakespeare Criticism.** Amsterdam 1979. 113p. 25,–
Contents: Introduction. Thomas Rymer: On *Othello* (1692). Nicholas Rowe: Preface (1709-14). Alexander Pope: Preface (1725). Lewis Theobald: Preface (1740). Samuel Johnson: Preface (1765). Richard Farmer: Essay on the Learning of Shakespeare (1767). Gotthold Lessing: On Ghosts (1769). Walter Whiter: On Hell and Night in *Macbeth* (1794). William Richardson: On the Faults of Shakespeare (1797). August Wilhelm von Schlegel: Lecture XXIII. Shakespeare (1809-11). Johann Wolfgang von Goethe: Shakespeare ad Infinitum (1812?). Samuel Taylor Coleridge: On Shakespeare as a Poet (1811-12). William Hazlitt: On Shakespeare and Milton (1818). Thomas de Quincey: On the Knocking at the Gate in *Macbeth* (1823). Thomas Carlyle: The Hero as a Poet (1841). Ivan Turgenev: Hamlet and Don Quixote: the Two Eternal Human Types (1860). Edward Dowden: Shakespeare's Portraiture of Women (1888). Walter Pater: Shakespeare's English Kings (1889). Bernard ten Brink: Shakespeare as a Comic Poet (1895). Richard Moulton: Supernatural Agency in the Moral World of Shakespeare (1903). Leo Tolstoy: Shakespeare and the Drama (1906). J.J. Jusserand: What to Expect of Shakespeare (1911-12). Sigmund Freud: On Lady Macbeth (1916). George Bernard Shaw: On Cutting Shakespear (1919). Edmund Blunden: Shakespeare's Significances (1929). Selected Bibliography.

New Series: Volume 16. **A.H. Qureshi: Edinburgh Review and Poetic Truth.** Amsterdam 1979. 61p. 15,–

New Series: Volume 17. **RAYMOND J.S. GRANT: Cambridge Corpus Christi College 41: The Loricas and the Missal.** Amsterdam 1979. 127p. 30,–
Contents: Chapter I: The Loricas of Corpus 41. Chapter II: Corpus 41 – An 11th-Century English Missal. Appendix: Latin Liturgical material contained in

the Margins of Cambridge, Corpus Christi College 41. Endnotes: Chapter I and Chapter II.

New Series: Volume 18. **CARLEE LIPPMAN**: **Lyrical Positivism**. Amsterdam 1979. 195p. 40,–
Contents: Chapter I: Some Tenets. Chapter II: The Rape of *The Rape of the Lock*. Chapter III: García Márquez' Language Laboratory. Chapter IV: The Syntax of Persuasion. Afterword. Bibliography.

New Series: Volume 19. **EVELYN A. HOVANEC**: **Henry James and Germany**. Amsterdam 1979. 149p. 30,–
Contents: Preface. Introduction. Chapter I: A Travel Sketch. Chapter II: The Analytic Tourist. Chapter III: Life Into Fiction. Chapter IV: Value, Inconsistency, and Resolution. Bibliography. Index.

New Series: Volume 20. **SANDY COHEN**: **Norman Mailer's Novels**. Amsterdam 1979. 133p. 25,–
Contents: Chapter One: Norman Mailer in Context. Chapter Two: The Naked and the Dead. Chapter Three: Barbary Shore. Chapter Four: The Deer Perk. Chapter Five: An American Dream. Chapter Six: History As Novel As History: Armies of the Night. Chapter Seven: Why Are We In Vietnam? A Novel. Chapter Eight: Marilyn. A Biographical Note.

New Series: Volume 21. **HANS BERTENS**: The Fiction of Paul Bowles. Amsterdam 1979. 260p. 50,–
Contents: Chapter One: Introduction. Chapter Two: The Sheltering Sky. Chapter Three: Let It Come Down. Chapter Four: The Spider's House. Chapter Five: Up Above the World. Chapter Six: The Stories. Chapter Seven: Conclusion. Selected Bibliography. Index.

New Series: Volume 22. **RICHARD MANLEY BLAU**: The Body Impolitic. Amsterdam 1979. 214p. 45,–
Contents: Preface. Chapter I. Typee: In Search of Plump Sphericity. Chapter II. White Jacket: To Scourge a Man that is a Roman. Chapter III. Moby-Dick: Beware of the Spinal Complaint. Chapter IV. Pierre: Let them look out for me now! Epilogue. Bibliography.

New Series: Volume 23. From Caxton to Beckett, Essays presented to W.H. Toppen on the occasion of his seventieth birthday, Edited by Jacques B.H. Alblas and Richard Todd. With a foreword by A.J. Fry. Amsterdam 1979. 133p. 30,–
Contents: List of Plates. Foreword. Acknowledgements. Hans H. Meier: Middle English Styles in Translation: A Note on *Everyman* and Caxton's *Reynard.* Richard Todd: The Passion Poems of George Herbert. Jacques B.H. Alblas: The Earliest Editions of *The Pilgrim's Progress* as Source Texts for the First Dutch Translation of Bunyan's Allegory. Peter J. de Voogd et al.: A Reading of William Hogarth's *Marriage à la Mode.* M. Buning: *Lessness* Magnified. A.J. Fry: On the Agonies of Elitism.

New Series: Volume 24. **CAROL JOHNSON**: The Disappearance of Literature. Amsterdam 1980. 123p. 25,–
Contents: Chapter One: The Disappearance of Literature. Chapter Two: Randall Jarrell and the Art of Self Defense. Chapter Three: Paul Valery: The Art of Concealment. Chapter Four: Hart Crane's Unimproved Infancy. Chapter Five: John Berryman: The Will to Exceed. Chapter Six: The Poetics of Disregard: Homage to Basil Bunting. Chapter Seven: The Translator as Poet. Chapter Eight: An Adjunct to the Poet's Dossier. Chapter Nine: The Consummation of Consciousness: The Poetry of Delmore Schwartz. Chapter Ten: Mrs. Wharton's Profession: The Reef. Reconnoitered. Chapter Eleven: Eça De Queiroz: The Arbitrations of Irony. Chapter Twelve: Nabokov's Ada: Word's End. Chapter Thirteen: Hysteria Naturalized.

New Series. Volume 25. **LINGUISTIC STUDIES offered to Berthe Siertsema**, edited by D.J. van Alkemade, A. Feitsma, W.J. Meys, P. van Reenen en J.J. Spa Amsterdam 1980. 382p. 56,–
Contents: D.J. van Alkemade: Referentiality and definiteness of NP's. D.M. Bakker: On *a*-generic sentences in Dutch. F. Balk-Smit Duyzentkunst: Metaphor and linguistic theory. R.A. Blust: Iban antonymy: a case from diachrony? S.C. Dik: On term coordination in functional grammar. A. Hurkmans: De Saussure and Wittgenstein. J.G. Kooij: Preposed PP's in Dutch and the definition of grammatical relations. P. Pitha: Case Frames of Nouns. S.R. Slings: 'KAI adversativum' – some thoughts on the semantics of coordination. E.M. Uhlenbeck: Observations in semantics is not easy. P.A. Verburg: Discipline versus philosophy. R. Botha: Allen's theory of synthetic compounding: a critical appraisal. H.H. Meier: Agnimals in English: group words in word groups. W.J. Meys: Morphemic make-up and lexical dynamics. Q.I.M. Mok: Le préfixe *RE*-re-regardé: productivité et potentialité. P. van Reenen/ J. Voorhoeve: Gender in Limbum. H. Schultink: On stacking up affixes, mainly in Dutch words. W. Zwanenburg: Regards du 17e siècle français sur la productivité morphologique. A. Cohen: The word as a processing unit in speech perception. A. Dees/ P. van Reenen: L'interprétation des graphies *-o-* et *-ou-* à la lumière des formes trouvées dans les chartes françaises du 13e siècle. H.D. Meijering: *D*(*e*)-deletion in the past tense of the class II weak verbs in Old Frisian. H. Mol: Gesture phonetics. J. Stewart: The feature Advanced Tongue Root and the Lepsius diacritics. J. Vachek: Writing and the glossematicists. B.P.F. Al: Sur la richesse lexicale du corpus d'Orléans. Contribution à l'analyse sociolinguistique d'un vocabulaire oral. J.T. Bendor-Samuel: Is a sociolinguistic profile necessary? A. Feitsma: The Frisian native speaker between Frisian and Dutch. G.J. Hartman: The goal-directedness of the process of sentence perception. E.A. Nida: The contribution of linguistics to the theory and practice of translating. J.J. Spa: Le langage et la sémiologie. Quelques réflexions nouvelles. B.T. Tervoort: What is the native language of a deaf child?

New Series. Volume 26. **FROM COOPER TO PHILIP ROTH**, Essays on American Literature, Presented to J.G. Riewald, on the occasion of his seventieth brithday. Edited by J. Bakker and D.R.M. Wilkinson, with a foreword by J. Gerritsen. Amsterdam 1980. 118p. 25,–

Contents: Foreword; T.A. Birrell: A Preface to Cooper's *The Last of the Mohicans*; A.J. Fry: *Writing New Englandy*: A Study of Diction and Technique in the Poetry of Emily Dickinson; D.R.M. Wilkinson: A Complete Image: James's *The Bostonians*; S. Betsky-Zweig: From Pleached Garden to Jungle and Waste Land: Henry James's Beast; J. Bakker: Faulkner's World as the Extension of Reality: *As I Lay Dying* Reconsidered; H.I. Schvey: Madonna at the Poker Night: Pictorial Elements in Tennessee Williams' *A Streetcar Named Desire;* G.A.M. Janssens: Styron's Case and "Sophie's Choice"; J.W. Bertens: "The Measured Self vs. The Insatiable Self:" Notes on Philip Roth; Curriculum Vitae; Publications; Tabula Gratulatorum.

Rodopi

Editions Rodopi N.V., Keizersgracht 302-304, Amsterdam, The Netherlands